SO DEEP IS THE NIGHT

BY

BRENDA FIELDING WOOLLARD

(The second part of her autobiography)

Published
by
Ian E.P. Woollard
TAMWORTH

First published in Great Britain on May 23rd 2002

by Ian E.P. Woollard

All photos from the private collection of B.F. Woollard except current portraits of herself taken by Ian E.P. Woollard

This book is available in paperback from the publisher at:-

Clifton Villas, 449 Glascote Road, Tamworth, B77 2BZ, England

All desktop publishing by Lorraine Jones of Tamworth.

Binding of this edition by Henry Mills of Birmingham

ISBN 0 9535471-1-6

INDEX OF CHAPTERS AND SETS OF PLATES

Brenda Fielding Woollard (nee Varley) was born in 1919. She was the fifth child of a family of six.

'So Deep is the Night' continues the story of her life where 'Farewell Asheton Schools' finishes. It tells of her eventful teenage years. First at her Fathers second school and then her various roles in the years leading to the second world war. Ultimately it gives the start of a love story between her and her 'beloved' Victor who she met and married when they were both in uniform. This love story was to last over fifty years and is a further story in the making.

-oOo-

In Loving Memory of my beloved husband Victor and for all our descendands

SO DEEP IS THE NIGHT

CHAPTER 1

OUR 'LITTLE HOUSE'

Half a mile from the village of St Michael's in the middle of Kent was a very large black and white striped house. This was my father's prep school for boys where I was born. It was the world I knew best until at the age of twelve life changed completely for me. I had to spend two terms at home doing lessons from time to time alone. Guided mainly by Mother or my eldest sister Winifred who was teaching at the time in our father's boy's prep school, known as The College.

I frequently took Peggy the dog for a walk. She was a pretty little dog, part collie but rather like a sheltie to look at. She belonged to Irene Budding who was matron at that time. In the school garden there was gym apparatus consisting of parallel bars, a vaulting horse and climbing ropes of various kinds. I spent much of my time on the ropes amusing myself climbing or swinging. I also had a swing fixed to the branch of a tree, which was very near to the gate through which we went when going between our 'little house' as we called it, at first, and the school. I spent endless hours on the swing, thoroughly enjoying myself.

In December 1930 when I arrived in the train that steamed into Broadstairs station, it was dark. I had one foot heavily bandaged and my legs raised along the seat in the carriage. A kind lady who was also travelling to Broadstairs had offered to look after me. We had been locked into our carriage by the guard so that I could keep my legs raised without disturbance.

My term times had been spent at a girl's boarding school in London for two and a half years, since the age of nine and a half. That morning I had been at a hospital having my feet probed by various doctors who were searching in vain for a small piece of needle that had entered my foot. The x-ray taken two days before showed it up plainly. Eventually they gave up and put eleven stitches in my foot. Mother and my brothers and sisters met the train. A chair was found for me to be taken to a taxi and my sister Sylvia gave me a pick-a-back up to the bedroom when we arrived at our new home.

This home was very different from the one I had left in September at the beginning of the term, where I was born and had lived ever since. My first home was the large boys' prep school in the middle of the country where my father was headmaster. We now had a smaller school but we also had a family home across the garden. It was the end of a row of houses each with four bedrooms, a bathroom and toilet upstairs, and a lounge, dining room, kitchen and scullery downstairs. My younger brother when told to get something from the larger, said he couldn't find the larder. The cupboard in the corner of the scullery was pointed out to him, whereupon he said, "What, that little cupboard?" We had had a large 'walk in' larder at our previous school, nearly as big as the scullery and kitchen put together in this house, and he couldn't understand that a cupboard could be called a larder.

My father lived in the school. Mother and the family lived in the 'little house' for nearly two years. By then two sisters, Sylvia and Dorothea and my elder brother Peter, were away from home. The rest of us, which meant my sister Winifred and my younger brother Michael, Mother and I, moved into the school.

I had not enjoyed being away at school, but even in my wildest dreams I did not think that I would never return. This however was to be the case as the doctor had recommended that I spend the next two terms running on the sands. He had taken me to the very new x-ray department at Margate Hospital, where film could be developed immediately after an x-ray. The piece of needle showed up. I was assured it was not likely to move and was unlikely to give trouble if left. I was given the choice of having it left, which I took, and where it has remained ever since without causing any trouble. I saw it on an x-ray about thirty years later. It was in three small pieces. My first view of the sea at Broadstairs was from a bath chair, made of basketwork. I was pushed by my sisters and brothers along the front, but not for long. I was soon running about as usual.

On Sundays whereas previously we had attended a Baptist Chapel, Mother decided that the 'Free Church of England' was preferable. Dr Magee who later became a bishop, was the minister there. We came to know him and his family as we went regularly. He had two daughters and a son. The boys in the school sometimes came with us but sometimes went to St Peter's Church.

Usually during the Easter holidays, hockey was played on the sands, though sometimes we used a field. The doctor's family and friends including some university students who joined us ran this. I had never played before but was allowed to if I hung about long enough. I was lucky if I hit a ball more than once in a game, so was not much use to the rest of the team, but I did enjoy it.

During the summer months 'Uncle Mack's Minstrels' performed daily on the beach and nightly in a very large tent on the jetty, where they had talent competitions. The tent was always packed and overflowing with holiday visitors as well as locals on talent nights. We rarely watched during the evening, it was too late, but I think even Mother came when my brother Peter entered and won with a recitation. It was a skit on Julius Caesar, which was very funny. There were two performances during the day, which I frequently watched. Mostly I stood near the back, though there were chairs. One of the minstrels came round with a collection box. As it came near me I tried to look as if I wasn't watching, I didn't have pennies to put into it!

In August there was a service in the tent on the jetty on Sunday evening at eight o'clock. We went to that sometimes. The Minstrels had a day of rest in those days and could sometimes be seen without their black make-up on, walking about the town.

There were regular donkey rides on the beach. I don't remember ever having a ride. It must have been the lack of pennies as well as the fact that I was getting rather too big to go on a donkey.

There was Dickens Week every year. There is a placard on the wall of 'Bleak House' where he wrote the book of that title. It is situated high on the cliff top not far from the jetty. During Dickens week many people dressed as some of his characters. Michael dressed up in a long tailed suit and a top hat but he didn't win a prize in the fancy dress parade that he entered.

Peter was away at T S Mercury most of the year. He had leave twice each year, six weeks in the summer and six weeks at Christmastime. He came home with many stories. How they all slept in hammocks and had to get up at six o'clock in the morning to scrub the decks. He told us that 'Ma Fry' who was in charge of the training ship always went for a swim in the sea every day and she was even then seventy years old. She was the wife of C B Fry the cricketer. Peter was keen on cricket too. He became head boy and returned home with his arms full of prizes he had won for all his good work. He first went there when he was twelve and said some boys were several years younger. Later he said that he thought it was wrong for such young boys to be sent where the life generally was so hard. He thought the age he had started there was quite young enough. I think Mother must have felt sorry for him. He was made a great fuss of by her when he was at home, staying in bed as late as he liked and on the whole doing as he liked. I didn't think that was a bit fair and regret to say I was jealous. During the holidays Peter joined the choir at St Peter's Church, where at that time, Edward Heath, known to us as Teddy, was head choirboy. He was just one year older than Peter. Peter sat next to him and Mother would refer to Teddy as 'that lovely good looking fair boy'!

In the summer Peter had his own small tent which he slept in on the lawn on a ground sheet, and when he got up he put everything he had in it in apple-pie order just as he had to do when he was at his training ship. Michael was still in school with the boys. On Sunday he was allowed to be 'at home', which meant coming to the 'little house' while we still had it, as he did in the holidays. He and I wandered round the garden together quite often, doing as we pleased. The garden was nothing like the previous one, which had eleven acres, two football fields, three large lawns, a big pond and plenty of shrubbery and kitchen garden. This one had a long drive boarded by tress and a small part with trees and shrubs near where, at the end of the rose garden the gym apparatus was.

There was also bluebell lane parallel to the drive, which ran along the bottom of the row of houses where our 'little house' was. It had hundreds of bluebells either side of a path, which we could walk through, or in my case frequently run through. The rose garden was a lawn where beds of roses were. A few acres had been made into a Japanese garden. There was a concrete man-made stream, over which one had to go via stepping stones. There was a Japanese house made mostly of bamboo and a rather dilapidated green house with some cactus plants in it. There was the remains of an aviary, which was not fit for use of any sort. Then there were various pagodas or statues made of stone. The boys were not permitted to go into the Japanese garden, but we went whenever we liked.

Behind the schoolhouse were greenhouses in which were grown grapes, peaches and nectarines. On an outside wall was a fig tree and upstairs in the house was a winter garden, which had many small black grapes in it. Some of our lessons were taken in there when it wasn't too cold. In the front of the house were various flower beds and boarders in which were irises and hydrangea bushes near the windows and a large circular rockery in the middle of the driveway opposite the front door. Then there was a large lawn, with a small sloping bank on one side. Beyond the lawn hidden by a hedge was a kitchen garden, and at the further side of the house near the back door were sheds and more greenhouses. There was also a lily pond, and further still up some steps a Dutch garden. The whole of the garden was scarcely more than half the size of the one we had been used to where we lived before.

We had a black and white cat called Jumbles in our 'little house' and there was a longhaired black cat in the school called Tinker, which belonged to Irene Budding. Apart from these cats, the dog Peggy that I took for walks and another one called Bob which belonged to Lewis Budding who was Irene's brother, we had no animals. We had had many where we were before. Mother, who was not, so to speak, an animal person at all, used to throw screwed up pieces of paper for Jumbles to play with, to stop him interfering with her knitting wool. She was at that time knitting a jumper for me. I think it was called random wool as it had a variety of colours, pink, red, white and so on that followed on at random. At an earlier age I had been taught to knit, but had not done any for some years. I decided I would knit a white jumper with short sleeves for myself. I had only ever done a plain stitch and didn't know how to follow a pattern so I taught myself to do pearl and did it backwards for many many years to come. It took me a whole year to make my jumper to my own pattern, which I was eventually very proud to be able to wear. This was followed by other jumpers while still in my teens and all to my own patterns.

During the first summer at Broadstairs, Mother's sister Auntie Elsie and Uncle Ronnie came to stay at a boarding house which was just next to one of our back gates that led out of the kitchen garden. Their daughters were at that time aged three, and one year. While they stayed there I had the job of fetching my two small cousins at seven in the morning to give Auntie and Uncle an extra hour or so of peace in bed. It was fine most mornings and the younger one Beryl was in a pram so we walked round the garden on the lawn. One morning however, it was wet so I took both children back to our 'little house'. The elder one Jean was soon occupied with a book sitting at the table in the kitchen, but I had to take Beryl out of her pram and put her down to crawl on the kitchen floor. While doing so she fell head first down the step that led from the kitchen to the scullery, onto the coconut mat which was there. She was not hurt but rather frightened so she screamed the house down! Because she had fallen on her head, I was terrified. I knew little about such small children but had had it instilled into me that baby's heads were delicate and must be treated with great care. I didn't dare to tell anyone and for a long time wondered what ill would become of her because she had fallen on her head. Needless to say my fear was quite unnecessary.

While we were in the 'little house' not much cooking was done. Most of our food came from the school kitchen and a lot of our meals we had in the school. Sometimes platefuls of dinner were put ready covered, one on top of the other, by our cook Emily and I would carry them wrapped in a cloth to eat with Mother at 'No 14' which was the 'little house'. Other times Emily would provide left over potatoes and greens and some raw eggs, which I soon found quite easy to fry in the dripping she would give me. Plenty of other provisions came our way from the school, as this was our only means of obtaining food. Mother didn't have money to buy food or anything else for that matter. We didn't go short. We could always have anything Emily had in the school larder, which was a narrow walk-in one, though not as large as the one we had had at the other school. There was at that time some burnt jam. I don't remember who burnt it or who made it but the general ideas was that it must not be wasted so had to be eaten before we had any other jam. If we got bananas and mashed them, then mixed them with the jam it was just about passable, so this is what we did until it was finished and we could have some more of another kind! We rarely had tinned food but we did have some tins of sardines, which although I didn't really dislike the taste of, I found they would always repeat after, so didn't like to eat them. Mother said that if I put pepper on them it wouldn't be so bad. I can't say I liked pepper, but I found it did help. When we had some brown bread, which we were not used to and most of us didn't like, she would say, "If you bite it up well it will taste like nuts." We found this rather a joke because we didn't really agree.

During the Easter holidays someone hit on the idea of walking to Sandwich. At least five of us went with out picnic lunches in little fawn cloth satchels. It was nearly ten miles each way. I had certainly never walked that far before but we took out time and really enjoyed the day. It was much talked of for a long time but not attempted again.

For the summer season we had a small canvas tent with a wooden floor. It was about four feet square and had just a flap that one could close by tying tapes together. It was amongst a number of rows of similar tents all privately owned, at one end of the beach. It was used purely for changing into or out of a swimming costume. I went swimming quite often, as did various others from our school and we usually left our clothes in the tent. Anyone could have got into it to help themselves but it just didn't happen. People were on the whole more honest at that time. Uncle Lewis, as we called him then, made good use of the tent. He could often be seen floating in the water but I don't think he ever actually swam. I never knew my father to swim at Broadstairs though he had done a lot of swimming earlier on. I spent a lot of time on the sands, sunbathing or playing generally, even building sandcastles or trying to beach comb without success. At least for the first two summers if not more. Watching Uncle Mack's Minstrels was often the highlight of the day as I could usually watch both of the daytime performances. I have the autograph of five of the Minstrels, by name 'Uncle Harry, 'Uncle John Hughes', 'Uncle Duggie', 'Uncle Jack', and 'Uncle Alex' but not 'Uncle Mack' himself. They were dated 1932.

CHAPTER II

'GROWING UP'

As well as all the greenhouses, we had a fern house at the college. This was always warm and damp. It was square with banks of ferns going up from a decorative iron grating path that surrounded a central rockery. Not only did all kinds of ferns grow there but also there were frogs to be seen quite often. Being on my own so much I frequently went into the fern house to see if I could find some. There was always water dripping through the ferns. Just before the end of the summer holidays, I was in the fern house one day when my father came in as he showed a visitor round with a prospective pupil. They were from the West Indies, so were coloured. Coloured people were rarely seen in our part of the world at that time, and although I took little notice of the short man, who, I found out later was a doctor and uncle to Roy the boy, I really warmed to Roy, in spite of the fact that he was some years older than I was and I was thrilled to think we would have a coloured boy in our school. My one experience of coloured people had been when I was only five or six years old. We had two Indian brothers who were students in our school then and they were both so charming they were very popular young men and I admired them too.

By the end of the summer my father had decided to have a few girls in the school for my benefit. The first to come was Edith. Her brother Brian who was younger was in the school too. Edith became a very special friend of mine for a long time. At first she slept in the same bedroom as I did at No 14, where previously Dorothea had slept. It had two beds and a chest of draws which we shared and a built in wardrobe, with plenty of room to spare for a couple of chairs at our bedsides. Edith was the same age as I. Her second name was Valentine and she liked to be called Val, but I always called her E-D-I. In that autumn term a couple of other girls came as well, as day girls, and we had lessons together, mostly in the library in the school, or the winter garden, or sometimes when Mother taught us, in the sitting room at No 14. Her special subject was French but she also took us for scripture and other subjects.

At midday until our main meal of the day at one o'clock we went for a walk and could go round the town or along the promenade by the sea, or where we liked. One girl, who lived in the same road as No 14, went home, returning for afternoon lessons from two until four.

About this time I was really growing up. When I said I thought I ought to wear what are now always referred to as a 'bra', I was sent to buy an all elastic one. It was about six inches deep and completely encompassed my chest, not the most comfortable of garments. It was not therefore long before I discovered there were much more comfortable ones to be had, and eventually was able to obtain one. Sanitary towels were always referred to, it they had to be mentioned, as 'S.Ts'. These were not bought in packets as they cost money, which was always in short supply. I have no idea what my sisters used; it was not something we talked about at all. I had towelling cloths similar to a babies' nappy and had to fold them and use pins. I then had to wash them and hang them on the clothesline, much to my embarrassment if anyone should see me. In fact quite soon I did all my own washing by hand in the bathroom basin. Also my ironing often in Mother's room. As long as lessons were attended and whatever preparation we were given, was done, life was mostly fairly free and easy. While still living at No 14 I ran over to The College on all kinds of pretexts when I fancied, frequently going into the kitchen where Emily would be, or through to their sitting room where she and her shell shocked bother Jesse, and Walter were. Jesse spent a lot of his time preparing vegetables and washing up for Emily. Walter was the houseman who did all sorts of things. They had the sitting room to rest in between their chores and to have their meals in during the day. In the evenings they returned to their own cottage which was not very far down the road through one of our back gates. Walter and Emily were good friends but he was about fifteen years younger. They lived in the same cottage but not as partners or any such thing and Jesse lived there too. Not so very many years later when Emily died I was told that Walter looked after Jesse for Emily. Jesse became a road sweeper and continued to work well into his eighties. Emily and Walter were good friends to me. I often spent time chatting to Walter when he was doing a job like cleaning the boy's shoes or sweeping a corridor. By hanging about like this I could see some of the boys, and the one I liked to see most was Roy. Gradually he and I saw as much of each other as we possible could, mostly in secret. One day we arranged to meet at the end of bluebell lane just near the gate that led into the garden of No 14, in the dark. That was the first of many times we managed to exchange kisses. How naive I must have been and I still laugh at the thought. I flew in after that first kiss to look in the mirror to see if the colour had come off on my face!

On arrival at Broadstairs my first Christmas had been spent at No 14, for the most part in bed, though I was carried down to the sofa on Christmas Day. The next Christmas was also spent at No 14. Just the family. All of us except my father. Winifred and Michael were at home as I was, though Winifred slept in the school, and my other two sisters had leave from their work. Peter was on leave too. Edith had gone to her grandparents for the holidays as her parents were in China. It was not long after that when No 14 was given up and we all went into the school to live. Mother had her own bedroom in one wing of the school. Edith and I shared a room further up the stairs from Mother's room, where there were three more rooms. We were two floors up. On the floor where Mother's room was there was a dormitory with beds for the five youngest boys in the school and a single bedroom. The first flight of stairs led from the hall to a landing where there were two bathrooms. They each had a bath in them. One had basins for the boys to use. The other was for staff and family. It had a fixed wash basin as well as a bath and a door to a walk in hot cupboard where linen was kept. There were lockers fitted to one wall of the bathroom where boys' clothes were kept. Up a flight of stairs to the other wing from where Mother's room was, one came first to my father's study come bedroom. There was a wide landing with lockers for boys' clothes, two dormitories and steps leading to the winter garden. There was also a ladies toilet. Up still yet another flight of stairs were two more dormitories and two private bedrooms. One was for a master and the other was where Winifred slept. My father exchanged his room for a dormitory, giving him more room. On the ground floor, on entering the front door there was a small room to the right usually called the drawing room. A large hall was straight in front, in which there was a grand piano. To the left was the main classroom and beyond also to the left, the library. To the right towards the back of the hall was the flight of stairs that led to where the bathrooms were. At the back of the hall was the dining room in which was an upright piano. This was used for assembly when it was held in the dining room. There were only about thirty boys in the school so there were two long tables for the boys and a large table in the centre where we girls sat for meals with members of the staff. Through the dining room was another classroom with a glass roof. It has been a greenhouse, and there was a covered way with a glass roof where the boys hung their coats and kept their shoes, in lockers under the coat hooks. There was also a classroom beyond the drawing room for the youngest boys, at the foot of more stairs that led to the bathrooms. At the back of the school was a rather dark passage which led from the hall near a staff toilet, round a corner to the top of the stairs that led to a lower level, where the kitchen quarters were. There were also boys' toilets, a washroom for the older boys and a door that the boys all used to go outside, at the end of the passage. Once outside a path led to a building known as the hut. It had been built at our previous school by the carpenter who was at that time the woodwork master in the school. It had been dismantled and rebuilt as an extra useful classroom and could be used for all kinds of things. The floor was wood. The walls were made of asbestos in wooden frames. If it was too wet for PE outside, this hut could be used. It was also where the school play was performed when a stage would be erected at one end. I will never forget the time I offered to help dress the boys who were may age, for the play. One boy was to wear a long dress that had belonged to my sister Winifred. I was helping him to put it over his head while he clutched at his trousers to keep them up, when suddenly in his effort to get both of his arms into the sleeves, he let his trousers fall. I was not used to seeing the older boys minus their trousers. I was too embarrassed for words. There were many things I joined in with at times that the boys did. One thing was target practice with tiny lead pellets. However, it didn't last long because the master, when loading a rifle managed to put a pellet into a boy's foot, when the rifle went off accidentally. My father put an immediate stop to it. This boy was one who had been in the same class as I had when I was still in school with the boys at home before going to boarding school. He was the boy who went riding every Saturday morning. I so loved the idea of being able to ride a horse, that I begged and begged to be allowed to have a ride. Eventually my father gave in and said I could have just one ride. Perhaps he thought he would cure me of wanting to ride. This was far from so however as I thoroughly enjoyed my one ride but I had quite a job to straighten my legs when I dismounted.

Mother's bedroom was much smaller than the one she had had at the previous school, so we no longer spent time in there playing games as we had done when we were all at home and much younger. She spent a lot of time in there as she had nowhere else much to go except when she was teaching, which was not very often, or having dinner with us. Most of her meals she had in her room. They were taken up to her. I popped in at times. She still had the very beautiful carriage clock in a case on her mantle shelf as she had always done. Also a china Dutch girl and a little white china cottage which was to put a night-light in. I don't know what happened to the Dutch girl, but Winifred had the clock, and Mother gave the cottage to my daughter at a much later date.

Mother suffered with curvature of the lower spine. It didn't show in any way. It was reputed to be as a result of a fall she had had in her teens. In spite of visits to various specialists it seemed that nothing could be done to help, so she had a constant backache. After the midday meal she always spent twenty to thirty minutes on her bed lying flat on her back as this was a temporary relief and when sitting had to have a cushion or a soft garment pushed into her back, to be comfortable.

One thing Mother always did in her bedroom was to gather together out-grown or unwanted clothes that still had plenty of use and make them into what was always known as a 'kind lady' parcel. It was then posted to a particular needy family and as she received a letter of thanks which was addressed to the 'Kind Lady', we adopted this name for the parcels.

When Mother had a friend to tea, which was not very often, she would use the small drawing room. On one occasion a friend brought some cream which we had for tea and I remarked that it was like velvet and that I liked it. I then asked for more! What a ticking off I had afterwards. Another time I had put on a blouse that I particularly liked, that had been cut from a dress. I wore a skirt with it that had been cut from another dress. I thought they looked really good together but was told in no uncertain terms that I could not come to tea in the drawing room 'dressed like that', so I said I wouldn't come to tea. I expect Mother despaired of me at times. I could be awkward and stubborn and that is to put it mildly. However, in my defence I must say that as I grew older, I was expected to be very grown up and responsible in many directions but was still treated as a child in others. I thought this was most unfair. I have no doubt though that I frequently behaved childishly. No one grows up all at once!

My father had school prospectuses that had to be sent by post to many people. I joined in helping to put them in the envelopes and then had to take them to the general post office. I enjoyed doing this. I was frequently asked to go in the evening to catch the last post with other letters as well, at half past eight. I ran all the way there and back, about a mile altogether. Another ticking off! It wasn't 'lady like' to run in the street. What a blow that was. I did so enjoy running and had little or no other opportunity. The prospectuses had a front cover in black and white of a picture of The College. I didn't think it looked very special. My father was an artist by nature. I rarely saw anything he did in the way of art because he didn't think anything he did was good enough. He had made an excellent job of the prospectus cover that had been used for our previous school. It was very colourful with masses of flowers in the borders in front of the school building, which was in itself very imposing.

The yo-yo became a new craze at that time. I had a smaller than average red wooden one. Some were made of tin and these days can be bought in plastic or other materials. I kept mine in my blazer pocket and played with it wherever I went. My blazer was worn most of the time except on Sunday. It was scarlet the same as the boys wore in the summer. We girls wore ours during the winter too with grey skirts and grey pullovers, white blouses and a red tie. We wore whatever stockings we liked. I had some black woollen ones that had been passed on to me by Winifred. She had had to wear them when she spent a year away at Ashford High School, before going to the London boarding school that we all went to. I tripped over an iron boot scraper that was on the step near the front door of the school when I was wearing them. I cut my leg but ignored it and finished with a round dent in my leg which was black and remained so for years to come. The black die had inbeded itself into the cut. I wore my hair long, which I had started to grow as soon as I knew I was no longer going back to the boarding school in London. I often plaited it into two plaits with ribbons at the end. Someone nicknamed them Swan and Edgar and I was often teased about them and had the ribbons snatched off. Eventually I had a large slide passed on to me by my sister Dorothea. It fitted comfortably into the nape of the neck and the hair was then loose down the back. Dorothea had her hair like that for some years but no longer did. I was then able to do so. At one time it was long enough for me to be able to sit on it. It was very thick and when brushed and combed it seemed to come out by the handful but still remained thick. It was customary at that time to have a hair tidy hanging on the side of the dressing table mirror. These were made of strong paper, shaped into a cone and coloured, then hung with a ribbon. Mine was soon filled and had to be emptied often.

I had been given a large doll that had a china head. It had been broken and sent to the doll's hospital. When it returned it didn't look the same so the owner no longer wanted it. I had always longed for a large doll with eyes that shut, so I was pleased to have it. However, I didn't appreciate it for long, I was getting too old to play with dolls. Walter said he had a six-year-old niece who would love to have it, so I gave it to him for her. He was most grateful.

Beyond the lily pond past the back door, there was a greenhouse that was used as a carpentry workshop. Uncle Lewis as we called him, had taken on the job of teaching carpentry in it. Then further still, there was a long rubbish heap that had been there some time before we arrived. This for some reason had to be transferred to what was known as the Dutch garden. Nothing very Dutch about it to my way of thinking, but the boys had their own gardens marked out, with paths in between. I remember Roy had cornflowers in his garden! This was also where the target practice was held while it lasted. The garden was square with walls on three sides, one of which was near the road. The fourth side had an iron railing fence with a gate in it. It had to be approached by going up steps and along a path. At the end of the path past the gate were high double doors that led out into the bottom of the road where No 14 was, but they were never used. In order to transfer the rubbish heap, a plank had to be put on the steps for a wheelbarrow to go up and down. I did a lot of wheelbarrow filling and pushing, and anyone else who wanted to, helped. Roy was one of these helpers. I enjoyed this chore, which was more of a game to me, and having Roy there helping was a bonus. We were not able to converse much as there were always others about, but I'm sure he volunteered because I was there and I know half the enjoyment on my part was his presence.

When the autumn came I spent a lot of time sweeping up leaves with a besom, a broom made of twigs bound to a handle. We had no official gardener. Various people did various things in the garden. At times the boys were formed into gardening parties to clear up parts of the drive and other places. Uncle Lewis mowed the lawns. He was the sort of person who could turn his hand to most things, from building or mending what we called a wireless to anything connected with his car as well as teaching boys carpentry. He was not our Uncle, but we called him that. He was Irene Budding's brother. My father, though not really a gardener as far as I know, once told me that if I dead headed the roses on the rose lawn whenever I saw one that had died, that they would boom until Christmas. I often went on or near the rose lawn so I frequently found a rose to dead head. As a result we always had roses up to Christmas time, every year. Uncle Lewis always saw to any of the electric's too. One day Peter thought he would play a joke. He went into the school by the back way to turn off the main switch at the meter in the meter cupboard, plunging the whole school into darkness. We were then, still living at No 14 so he fled back afterwards. Uncle Lewis soon found out that the switch had been turned off, and twigged that it was Peter. He went at once to No 14, found Peter, and told him what he thought of him. Peter was so taken aback at being found out so quickly that he tried to make out he was not responsible. Peter was promptly given a 'thick ear', which I witnessed as I was there at the time. He was then told that it was for not being truthful. Uncle Lewis, usually a mild man, was absolutely livid! I don't think Peter had any sympathy from anyone for his 'thick ear', and I rather think it was the last time he told a fib, as we always used to call it!

I was about a year older when I went swimming every day. In fact one year my sister Dorothea, or Thea as we all called her by then, and one of Dr Magee's daughters and I, went in the sea every day. The idea was to see if we could do it for a whole year. Actually I was the only one who kept it up though they were not far behind. Towards the end of completing the year I would go running down through the back gate of the garden, which was nearest to the sea, in the early morning wearing a raincoat over my bathing costume and a towel round my neck, by myself. Leaving sandals, raincoat and towel on the sands, I plunged in and out all in the space of less than two minutes and ran home again to have a hot bath. I was so determined to be able to say I had been in the sea for every day for one year. There were no tents on the sands when I made my solitary sojourn and almost no one about, except perhaps the occasional person walking a dog up on the promenade at the top of the cliff. When it was warmer I often went at any time of the day, sometimes with others but often alone. Then I would use the tent and if possible choose when the tide was in. I could then plunge in and get completely wet immediately and swim right across the bay to the jetty, where I could get out at the steps, run all along the jetty and back along the waters edge on the sands to the tent.

We had a lot of tents in the garden during the summer. Peter had his own on the big lawn and slept on a ground sheet using blankets and a pillow as the only bedding. There were various other tents on both the big lawn and the rose lawn. Most had camp beds in them. In the holidays, on wet days we often spent quite a lot of time in them, chatting or doing nothing in particular. We had plenty of boys and some girls who stayed during the holidays. They came from all kinds of places, including many from abroad. They were not necessarily out term time schoolboys or girls, though some were. Two brothers about our ages were German. Three brothers who had parents in Malaysia and a cousin of theirs were all our schoolboys. Many I do not remember, but the middle one of the three brothers said something in Malay to Peter as he had learned some Malay and had taught Peter. I asked what he had said as he had been looking at me, and grinning. Peter told me he had said, "Shall I kiss your sister?" and Peter had replied, "Yes, if you like." I was only twelve at the time and although not very interested I was quite flattered that he should want to kiss me. I promptly received a peck on the cheek to which I made no objection but it was not repeated and the mutual affection petered out without any animosity on either side. Some of the tents were home made with treated calico that had been stitched to fit frames that Uncle Lewis made. I think he machine stitched the calico himself too. They were all right for showers if the inside wasn't touched but not really a lot of good if the rain was heavy. I sometimes slept on the ground but mostly on a camp bed. One year, after most people had gone home or back to their beds indoors, I thought I'd stay out in the tend all the winter. My tent was not on, but near to the rose lawn under some trees. The tent post blew down several times and I had to put a ground sheet, which was rubber one side and some sort of cloth the other, on top of my bed to keep the bedding dry, when the rain came in. I found Michael had fixed the pole up for me on one occasion. Sometimes I found the cat was on or even in the bed when I went out to go to bed. I even kept my coat on a few times and always had a sweater on over my pyjamas and wore bedsocks. I was very pleased to go back up to the bedroom where by then, my bed was in the room where Winifred slept.

Plate Titles

Section One

1) 1930. My younger brother Michael, aged nine

2) 1930. Girls on day trip to Rottingdean from boarding school in London.

3) My second cousin Joan Varley on the left in both photos. Her mother was Headmistress of the school.

4) 1930. A friend and me on the Rottingdean trip.

5) 1930. 'Tootles', belonging to 'Uncle and Auntie'.

6) 1931. Mother and the family outside the front door of The College. Me on the left.

7) The family taken at the same time with Mother.

8) 1931. Cousin Jean, known as 'Snowball' because of her white outfit, seen here on the sands at Broadstairs.

CHAPTER III

EARLY TEENS

In the middle of Broadstairs was, and I think still is, a Park, called Piermont Gardens. It was where fetes were sometimes held. We didn't go there often but on one occasion I was there at a fete when I entered a running competition. I could run or so I thought, as I did whenever I had the chance. I had however, had no competition and was amazed to find myself coming in last but one. What a blow to my ego! It was not a big park but I was very surprised to find it had a drinking fountain in it. I had only ever seen a drinking fountain in London and Hastings.

We had a fete, one year in our own garden on the big main lawn. I don't remember what it was in aid of. I was given a tray with bags of home made sweets on it and asked to walk round asking people to buy them. One man who was an acquaintance of Mother's, from the church, asked me how much it would be for the whole tray full. When I told him, he gave me the money and then told me to keep the sweets for myself. I had never seen such generosity. I was flabbergasted!

As time went on so many things seemed to change. At Christmas time in the school there were plenty of people and children who were not family. My father mostly gave other children much the same as he gave us. One year we all had a jar of sweets. Another year everyone had a book. Some years before, we six children had a picture each. They were called 'Cries of London'. Mine was of fish being sold. We were frequently given books for all sorts of occasions. I still have a book of 'Poems by Tennyson'. Given to me by my Father for my thirteenth birthday. I have never read much of it except perhaps 'The Charge of the Light Brigade'. I never have been keen on poetry. In the book my Father wrote, "Tennyson was a great Englishman, and like most great men, a man of many words, yet he never wrote anything unkind or base." One lovely book called, 'The Book of Elves and Fairies' that he gave me one Christmas, I had for about twenty-five years or more. I lent it but it was never returned. I still have 'The Tale of Mr Tootleoo' a quite amusing book, given to me by my Father when I was eleven, and 'The House of Fancy' which is a lovely book, dated 1922.

On Boxing Day, it was the one day in the year when we could get up when we liked. There must have been other presents given to me which I don't recall but I always took a delight in writing 'Thank you' letters on Boxing Day and some would be written before I was up and out of bed, and the rest before the day was out. I liked writing letters particularly if I had been given a present of writing paper.

When I was thirteen, Mother's younger sister our favourite Auntie, known as 'the jolly Aunt', died. She was in her early forties. My sister Sylvia who had not long started her nursing training visited her. Auntie Pixie as we called her asked Sylvia what was written on her record sheet, as she didn't know what was wrong with her, and didn't understand the medical terms. Sylvia couldn't tell her, as she didn't understand either. She said later that she was glad she didn't understand at the time, as she would not have liked to be the one to tell her she had cancer. At that time it was a very taboo word. No one other than those in medical circles ever mentioned the word. Auntie Pixie was given radium treatment but it was not of any use.

We children were not allowed to visit her, as she knew how ill she looked and preferred that we remembered her as she had been. We always spoke of and thought of her as the 'Jolly Aunt'.

At about that time we used to have 'Lobby Ludd' on the front at Broadstairs. If you had the right paper under your arm you could go up to him and say, "You are Mr Lobby Ludd, I claim the .... prize." The name of the paper had to be mentioned but I am not sure which one it was. I often looked for him but I didn't have the paper. Some people must have found him and won the money prize that was given. I think quite a lot of men, who were not Lobby Ludd, must have been challenged, and some must have been quite fed up with it, and the challengers must have often been disappointed!

When I wanted to have a holiday away from home, it was arranged for me to go to stay with 'Auntie' at 'Water's Land'. She wasn't a real Auntie but lived down the road from where we used to live and we often spent time in her house when we lived near. A niece of hers, Vera, about my age, whom I had met before, lived a few miles from us in Broadstairs. Vera went to visit 'Auntie' at the same time. We had a lovely time, not doing anything of very special note, except for taking her dogs for walks or helping to feed the chickens. 'Auntie' and 'Uncle' had a smallholding and we both just loved to be with 'Auntie'. She was always kindness and sweetness itself. Never was a cross word uttered by her. We were sometimes able to help make cakes, but not expected to do a single chore. They also had 'Grandad' living with them. He was 'Uncle's' father and a nice 'old chap' we thought.

One summer some boys developed scarlet fever. They had to be sent to the Isolation Hospital which was over three miles away out of the town and into the country, not so very far from Manston aerodrome. It was one morning when I was supervising the younger boys, who were aged about seven years old, when they were getting up. First one, then another and then a third boy said his back itched. I told Mother, who said they had scarlet fever and that they must go back to bed and she would arrange for them to go to the hospital. As I had been with them I was told to take cups of tea to them but that no one else should go near them. When the ambulance came for them they went in pyjamas and dressing gowns and all their bedding had to be taken to be fumigated as well. It was discovered later that someone had the infection in their tonsils, we were told, but he didn't get the disease, and neither did I. A few older boys had already had it as well, but only about six from the school altogether. Some weeks later when they were getting better I had to walk all the way to the hospital carrying a case full of clothes for them. Then when they were well enough to return to school, I had to go yet again with some more clothes. There was no such thing as a bus going that way. It was hot sunny weather so that walk was no joke! Although I often volunteered to do things, I'm sure I didn't volunteer to do that walk twice, it was not something I enjoyed doing.

The supervising of the younger boys getting up and going to bed was something I am sure I volunteered for as I enjoyed that immensely and never minded getting up extra early in order to do it. We always had to go to bed early so I was wide-awake quite early. I was able to have a bath every morning but it had to be very quick, as others wanted to do the same. The water was always hot and a bath had to be followed by what Mother called 'a cold swill'. This meant dashing cold water over neck and chest before drying with a towel. It was Mother's way of keeping healthy. "It makes you 'all of a glow'", she would say. I'm not sure how much good it did, but I grew out of doing it some years later! The hot water was so hot the pipes became silted up with chalk and burst one day swamping the downstairs boys' washroom where the boiler was. The coke for the boiler was kept outside on a huge concrete slab over the top of what was known as the coalhole, where the coal was kept, as we had coal fires in a few rooms. The coal had to be kept dry. The coke burned better if wet, so it was left open to the rain. In dry weather it had to be dowsed with buckets of cold water. Some of it was used in with the coal on fires as the coke was cheaper and we always had to economise. Walter dealt with the boiler and the fires. We also had paraffin stoves for heating in the classrooms, and Mother had a paraffin stove in her bedroom.

For one term when both Mother and Winifred were not well, I had the job of teaching six small boys for most of the term. I was only fourteen at the time but looked older. One of them I was in the habit of fetching before nine o'clock in the morning for school. It only took about twenty minutes if, as I usually did, I ran all the way across the allotments to his home and with him in tow back again and through the back gate at the bottom of the kitchen garden. While I was teaching I still had to fetch him each morning but I never had to take him home. These boys were all about six years of age, and mostly boarders, except the one I fetched and one other. This other one was rather a solemn, pale faced little boy, and as dim as they come. I felt very sorry for him. One morning he didn't arrive as usual for school, so inquiries were made. There was no one at his home. It was found later that the whole family had gone. No one knew where to but they left behind many unpaid bills, so it was said and of course school fees were owing too.

After that term of teaching I went back to my own lessons with the aim of taking the matriculation exam a couple of years later. However, that was not to be. I did one more year of English, French, German, Latin, History, Geography and Maths. I still have some of the exercise books. I did many of the back numbers of the matriculation Maths papers, and managed fairly well, but anything else that I tried I was never very much good at. Michael at the age of only thirteen did a matriculation geometry paper and obtained 100%. He was always wizard at Maths. We were taught by Winifred as often as not. By then there were about six of us girls in a class. We didn't have lessons with the boys, except sometimes for Maths when the door between the class of boys and the library where we were was opened and Winifred taught us altogether. We varied in age so it was not easy for whoever taught us. Reg Hitch was a master who taught us German. A second cousin of ours who came to help when I was about thirteen or fourteen married him. He was twenty-eight and until then had always insisted he was a confirmed bachelor. Beryl, our cousin was only slightly younger but she had married an Egyptian and gone to live in Egypt some years before. She returned, thoroughly disillusioned with the way of living in Egypt. She had with her an eighteen-month-old daughter, Fayza. While helping in the school in the dining room she had a young girl who had just left school to come to take Fayza out for a few hours each day. After a while it didn't work out very well. She and Reg were then married and were happy for many many years. Reg later taught in another school in Broadstairs, where he taught the then, young Royals.

By the time there were quite a few girls, we had moved into The College and two or three were daygirls. I don't think there were ever more than seven, at one time. There were some rules that had to be kept, but we were often allowed to go out to wherever we liked. We could walk as far as the stables which was quite a distance but there was no village blacksmith to watch as he put shoes on the horses, so at first we didn't go very often. We could visit the new houses that were being built where fields had been. In fact we would sometimes go into the houses that were nearly finished but had no outside doors. There was a big board to say they could be bought for seven hundred pounds. I thought it would be good to save up enough to buy one. I can't imagine how I thought I would save that amount. We often went down into the town or along the front. If I was asked to buy something at one of the bigger shops, I would be told to have it put on the account. One shop where that could be done was the chemist, and one thing I was sent to ask for more than once was a particular cough mixture. It was a prescription that had probably been made up by my Uncle Edwin who was a chemist. It had ipecacuanha wine in it. "And be sure to ask to have the prescription back", I was told. With our own money we could sometimes buy twopennyworth of chips in newspaper, but we never had enough money for fish as well.

If, as we often did, we went out of one of the back gates we would go past 'Bohemia'. It was a hall where all kinds of shows were held, mostly in the evenings especially during the summer. What a noise would come from there. There was a girl, whom we never did get to know. She was known as my double. I only saw her a couple of times but a number of different people would tell me from time to time that they had seen my double.

There was, for a time just one shop left with the overhead wires going from the assistant behind the counter, where a little pot could have money put into it and sent overhead to the cash desk, which was a very small closet, with glass nearly all round it, through which the cashier could be seen. When the cashier received a pot, she would take the money out and return the pot with a receipt and if necessary some change. Other shops had previously done away with them. We still saw horses wearing blinkers, pulling a cart, or sometimes stationary with a nosebag on having its feed, snorting and snuffling as it ate and tossed its head from time to time. We rarely went on a bus or tram, but as trams went to Ramsgate we would occasionally go by tram. Sometimes, though not very often we would walk all the way to Ramsgate. It was about three miles and took about forty minutes.

There were no longer any vehicles with solid tyres. If it was wet, going on the top of the tram or bus had to be avoided if at all possible, as they were often open topped. Some open topped vehicles had canvas covers to spread across from seat to seat to keep the wet out, but they were not very satisfactory.

When the sea was rough, one delight was to walk down to the jetty and go along to the end to try to dodge the spray from the sea as it came right up over the top and sometimes off down the other side. We had to wear suitable clothing, as we didn't always manage to dodge the spray.

In the summer when it became fashionable to wear beach pyjamas, I went to the beach in mauve and white striped pyjamas that I usually wore in bed. They were boys' pyjamas. I thought I was 'the cat's whiskers' as I walked down the street. I was soon told that they were quite unsuitable, but I didn't think that they were any more unsuitable than those worn by others on the beach. I wore sandals all the summer except on Sunday, if I possibly could, as once I had a pair I found them so comfortable I didn't want to wear anything else.

My father on the odd occasion would include me when taking a small party of people to the cinema, much to Mother's disapproval. I enjoyed a film about Disraelli, and once I had seen Clark Gable on the screen, I had to have his picture on my bedroom wall. I thought he was 'the tops'. Mother didn't often disapprove openly of things my father did, but on one occasion she was horrified. It was while we still had No 14. I went through the dining room, which was a short cut to get there. My father was sitting at the table alone having his supper, so I stopped to talk to him. There was a bottle of burgundy on the table and some was in a glass from which he was drinking. I asked him what it tasted like. "Try it" he said, and handed the glass to me. I took a tiny sip. Ugh! The one and only time I ever tried it and thought it was horrible. When I went in to say 'good-night' to Mother she asked me what I had had. I told her exactly what had happened. I then had a real ticking off and was told never to taste any such thing again. I felt that, that was grossly unfair and considered that if my father had given his permission that it was perfectly in order. It was, I suppose, just as well that I didn't like it, as I had no wish to try tasting anything like it for years. I rather think there was method on my father's part. He had guessed I wouldn't like it.

There was another walk we quite often took together. We girls, that is. That was to the home of Diana Ostra. She was a day pupil. Her younger brother Tony was a weekly boarder. She had keys and seemed to know when no one would be at home. She always had plenty of money so could buy sweets and bars of chocolate as and when she liked. She could also put things on account in some shops. She was most hospitable and generous to us. She and her brother were both by lingual as they had spent some time in France. These walks were taken during the day between eleven and twelve or between twelve and one o'clock, when we went out for our hour of fresh air. We had no official games or PE so it was our one time for exercise. But there were many times if it was not wet when I did hand stands and performed other antics on the lawn. Then there was the swing and the gym apparatus and the vaulting horse, with the springboard. I could sometimes persuade someone to catch me if I vaulted free over the horse, which was great fun.

There were plenty of times when I went on my own to shops or even to visit Emily and Walter in the evening in their little cottage. I was always welcome. Broadstairs was a very safe town. Anyone could be out alone at night without any fear, and one often saw a local policeman on his beat. As the daughter of a local headmaster many people knew me or should I say, knew who I was without my knowing who they were, so I had to make a point of behaving. This meant that I could not be seen out with my boyfriend Roy that I was supposed not to have as a boy friend. In spite of the fact that we loved each other very much. So our solution was to meet at Emily's little cottage where she would let us sit by her fire. We were careful not to be seen either arriving or leaving together. We knew we could rely on both Emily and Walter not to let anyone know.

Even after going to live in the school, when there was no need for me to go into the kitchen like I had done when we were living at No 14, I often went to chat to Emily. I would watch her cooking. I no longer needed even to cook supper, or had the chance to. Sometimes she would be laboriously mixing butter and margarine together. The margarine was so much cheaper than butter that it was an economy that was almost essential. No one seemed to mind. There were other times when I enjoyed watching Walter as he distempered the dormitories. I learned a lot from him about decorating, which served me well in later years. Walter was mostly very respectful, keeping his place as the houseman, and always calling me 'Miss Brenda'. However, he once caught me under the mistletoe! I was in a way flattered, but from then on I was on my guard making sure he didn't try it on again. He could be a tease at times. There was a boy called Dennis Storey, a few months older than I. He was a dayboy and seemed to come and go as he pleased when it was not lesson time. There were very few dayboys, the others were younger. Dennis, always called Storey as boys were called by their surnames, and I, seemed to be around somehow together quite often, for no particular reason. If I was alone, Walter would tease me to try to annoy me by saying, "Where is your Sheik today?" meaning Dennis Storey, just to watch me blush to the roots of my hair, which I did easily and often, and to hear me either ask him what he meant, or hotly deny that I had a Sheik, when I knew that he meant Dennis. There was in fact nothing between us except for a sort of fraternal, almost love hate relationship. However, Walter was either not, or pretended not to be convinced, and I never knew quite which, and my boyfriend Roy whom I really loved was always jealous if he saw us together, so I had to be careful as he was not convinced that Dennis meant nothing to me. There was one thing Walter was good for when the grapes and peaches and nectarines were ripe. If I saw him in the greenhouse and there was any ripe fruit to be had, I could usually get some from him, but although he tended them by pruning, thining out or watering as and when necessary, he had to be careful in case he was accused of helping himself. There was usually plenty but I was sworn to secrecy, no one must know he gave my any, and he knew he could trust me. The grapes were never very big but there were black as well as white ones. A lot of them were in the Winter Garden as it was called, which was used as a classroom or sitting room by various people. I sometimes sat with others doing my knitting and at one time I had Mother's sewing machine in there. I think she seldom used it by then, though she had made dresses and such like on it when we were younger. I managed with a great effort on my part to cut out and sew on the machine two blouses for myself. Quite an achievement for me as I really didn't excel at or even enjoy sewing. There was quite a lot of room in the Winter Garden and as it was all glass it was very light and often too hot in the summer or too cold in the winter. It was situated immediately over the dining room and in the centre was a raised rectangular glass surrounded by a railing. The glass let the light into the dining room below. Another place we could often go into was the library. It was like a sitting room but had library books on shelves all along one wall. There was also a piano, arm chairs and a table in there. Sometimes we had tea by the fire and made toast with a long pronged fork, by holding the bread which was fitted on to the prongs, to the fire when it was glowing suitably, and we had to turn the bread to the other side, once one side was done.

Two of our masters were brothers, who had been in our previous school as pupils. Jack the elder one came first after he had been in Africa. He suffered from time to time from malaria. He had a bedroom in our little house for a while. This meant he had to be looked after when he had high fevers. Mother did most of that but just occasionally I had to take a cup of tea to him. I don't know what he taught. He had very thick glasses and was not the sports master. His brother, Jerry came as sports master. He was an artist. I couldn't make out or understand some of his pictures, so I made, not very polite remarks about them. I was then told I was ignorant and obviously couldn't appreciate good art! However, we didn't fall out over it. I liked both Jack and Jerry, as did most other people.

Jerry was not with us long. Jack was for quite a time. Winifred was teased about Jack as we thought she was particularly fond of him. That stopped when he introduced Eileen to us and we soon came to know her quite well. Not long after, their baby Anthea was born in the summer of 1934. There was another master, a Mr White but I remember very little about him. We had a very popular French master. He was known as Monsieur Pithard and we knew him for some years. We later called him by his first name Georges. He was very tall and his eyesight was not good. He tried very hard to learn all the English he could, but no matter how hard he tried and with all our help, he could not acquire a good accent. Everyone was very sorry when he left and a number of us received postcards from him afterwards. Many years later Winifred told me that he still lived in France in the same place which I think was Dieppe, as I believe she visited him once, but as he grew older he became blind.

Health in the school was generally good in spite of the scarlet fever. Boys were still measured and weighted at the beginning and end of term as they had been at Asheton, which was our previous school. One boy who often looked pale and was not very robust was ill a few times until a grumbling appendix was diagnosed, then he had to have an operation. He seemed much better once he had recovered from that. If I needed to see the doctor, which was rare, I went alone. I had no wish to have Mother come with me and I am sure she had no wish to accompany me. If as I often did, I went to the dentist, I also went alone, and was quite happy to do so.

While we were still at No 14, I think Mother was not very happy. I think she felt isolated. On one occasion I actually found her shedding tears, which rather shocked me at the time. Although she did a little teaching, which she loved to do, she was not involved in any matron's or other duties.

There were a few occasions when we would have some sort of party, or someone to tea, particularly when any of the family who were away, returned for a short while. Dorothea was good at doing a little sketch called 'Can't blow the candle out'. It was about a family who all had peculiar mouths so could not blow the candle out and she acted each one as she told the story. Then she ended by saying, "I could blow the candle out, but next time you find it difficult just do this," whereupon she licked her thumb and forefinger and pinched it out. This always went down well. Others did other things but not I. I was not a performer in any shape or form. Sometimes at teat time a game would be played. When one day we were supposed to act the title of a book of some sort in some way, one person picked up a spoon from the table and put it in the buttonhole of his jacket lapel. He said the book was called 'The Silver Spoon' but no one else had ever heard of it!

We had no phone at No 14 but there was one in the drawing room in the school. It was very rarely used. I answered it a few times and then had to fetch my father to speak to someone. With permission I made the odd very rare call. There was a box with a handle on the side, on the window sill, which had to be wound to call the operator and then a trumpet like piece had to be taken from the side of the stand where the speaker was, to be put to the ear and the call made through the operator.

Bad language was heavily clamped down on. I once referred to someone as a nincompoop and another time a twerp and received a reprimand from Mother both times. The worst thing Mother ever said was 'bother' and I once and only once heard my father say 'botheration'. That was the extent of his 'bad' (!) language. At the time I was very surprised but somewhat amused, I had never heard the whole word like that before! The masters were mostly very good about not letting anyone hear bad language from them and boys knew punishment would be handed out if they dared to use words they soon came to know were not permissible. Boys were never allowed to walk about with their hands in their pockets. My father never did. He very frequently walked with his hands behind his back and at times would stand holding the lapels of his jacket. He never tied his tie; it was always threaded through a gold finger ring that had belonged to his Grandmother or some such.

The holiday I had at Auntie's with Vera was not the only time I went there. I had another time there not long after on my own. I think Uncle Lewis must have taken and fetched me as he used his car to our advantage a lot. No one else could drive and I know he quite liked to visit Auntie and Uncle, as they were always called. I used to do messages for Auntie to the village shop, and had a ride with her in the donkey and trap when she wanted to go all the way into Tenterden, which was about two miles. It was odd to be back near where I had lived for so long but not to go into the house or garden, but just to go past. Not much had changed. The farm opposite what had been our school was still there and their chickens were all over the road just as they had always been, as we went by. There was always plenty to do at Auntie's. I loved to help. She was always so grateful for any help, whether it was taking the dogs George and Colin out for a walk, feeding the chickens or collecting eggs or picking the rabbit food in the lanes. And she let me make cakes which I really enjoyed doing.

Plate Titles

Section Two

9) 1932. Jean's sister Beryl aged one year, on our lawn.

10) 1931. H.V. by the rockery at The College.

11) 1932. Edith in chair with her brother Brian and Jane.

12) 1932. Beryl Varley on the beach with baby in pram at Broadstairs.

13) 1930. (approx) H.V.

14) 1933. Me in school blazer.

15) 1933. Jack Morris with Edith wearing a blazer.

16) 1933. Roy in the Japanese garden.

CHAPTER IV

ROY BROKE HIS LEG

All the time we were at Broadstairs Winifred was a teacher in the school. She had started to teach as soon as she left school herself, at our previous school. I think her main subject was Maths. She certainly took the girls for Maths. She also taught some other subjects to all ages. Mostly we liked her classes and I think the boys did too. I saw her quite often in between lessons and later on shared her bedroom. We got on well.

Sylvia was quite different. When she first left school which was two terms after Winifred she started to teach in the school at Asheton. It lasted no time at all. My father said she was too lenient with the boys which when I think about it rather surprises me. I knew she could be and often was a buffoon, but when being serious always struck me as being too strict, and in any case, in her book she was always right. She was soon away from home and didn't teach at Broadstairs at all as far as I remember. She went to live with our

Grandparents in North London to what the family always referred to as 'West Bank' which was the name of the road, which went along the west side of the railway line opposite to where they lived. There were two Aunties still living there too. Sylvia seemed very happy living there with them for about two years while she worked in an LCC office. I have no idea what the work was, but she was never interested in having a boyfriend of any sort. When she was much younger she had been teased about one boy at home but there was never anything in it and for years she used to tell us that when she retired she would marry a rich farmer! At the age of twenty she started her nursing training at Hackney Hospital and continued until she had full qualifications including midwifery. She went out on the district into the poorest of homes, but worked in another London hospital all through the war. She came home to visit whenever she was free at first. She was good at writing letters so always kept in touch and I always wrote to her too.

Dorothea had left school at a younger age than Winifred or Sylvia. In fact she left when Sylvia did. She was fourteen and insisted that she could study for her School Certificate exam by doing a correspondence course at home. This she did, took her exam and passed. That was the end of her schooling. She was by then very nearly fifteen. She may have taught for a short time, I am not sure and she may have taken another job for a time. But while we were at Broadstairs she spent two or three years at Westgate. She enjoyed her job there as governess to some children in a private home run by two middle-aged spinsters. She taught and looked after children who had well to do parents some of which were abroad. Dorothea came home often when she had time off. Westgate was only five or six miles from our home. Uncle Lewis transported her back and forth whenever she liked. In fact during those years they spent a lot of time together and were much talked about! Uncle Lewis was about thirty years older than Dorothea. By the time Dorothea was about eighteen, she thought she would follow Sylvia and started a nursing training at Hackney Hospital where Sylvia was. However this only lasted about three months as she contracted rheumatic fever and came home to converless after being very ill for a time. It was said that it was caused by the dampness of the nurses' home where she had to live while training. This put an end to her nursing career.

During the summer she was a waitress in a café in Perranporth in Cornwall. Then she was at home part of the time, and by the time she was twenty she was at Monkton Wyld, which is another story to come later.

Peter was at the T S Mercury most of the time we were at Broadstairs, but before we left he had finished his training and went into the Royal Navy as an A B. He was posted to Chinese waters. There was by then a lot of unrest in China. I was convinced he had gone there to be killed. I wrote to him. He wrote home, but there were times when I shed tears on my pillow because I thought he would never return. Before he left when we knew he would be gone for at least two years, we were able, with great difficulty and much persuasion to have a photograph taken of all eight of us. It was wonderful in later years to look at and harp back, so to speak, but in many ways it was the end of an era. We were never all together again.

Michael was still in school with the boys at Broadstairs until he was thirteen. Then he went to the public school St Lawrence College at Ramsgate. He was there about two years. He went as a dayboy cycling the two miles or more there and back each day and at one time outgrew his strength because he became so tall, all of a sudden.

During these years I was in the girl's class at home and gradually took on many duties. Mother would at times get quite irritated with us and go very red in the face if she was extra annoyed when we didn't behave as she thought we ought. Behind her back, we girls would indulge in ribald sarcasm, mock her and say she was 'ratty'. Just as well she never knew that. We often spent a lot of time giggling which we knew annoyed her, and I rather think I was the biggest culprit when it came to giggling! However, we did grow out of it and as time went on learned to behave and take life more seriously.

On one or two occasions my father had good reason to do what we called 'read the riot act' to us in his study. I made a point of telling the others that it paid not to say a word unless asked a direct question, because I had learned from previous lectures that if anyone said anything, a second lecture would be forthcoming. These occasions were very rare. My father could be a stern headmaster but he was a very loving father. When I was much younger I stood in awe of him. It had always been expected of us that after morning assembly or any other time if it was the first meeting of the day, that we should exchange a kiss or 'peck' on either cheek, French style. Mother expected this from us too, and it continued throughout their lives. However, I must say that during my teens I sometimes received what I would then call a proper kiss as opposed to a 'peck' from my father, which I must admit, pleased me enormously.

Once we were all in the school, Mother decided to run a Sunday afternoon class, something like a Sunday School. We were expected as family to attend, so we did and any of the boys or girls in the school could if they chose to, but no one found it compulsory. It took the form of prayers, Bible readings, hymns and a talk, lasting about an hour. We often had a chance to choose a hymn. Mother, who was by way of being a home evangelist if ever there was one, would give the talk. Auntie Birdie, a very special friend of Mother's who had been a missionary in Syria and who came to stay a few times, would give us the talk while she was with us. We had been brought up as a Christian family and had always been taught we were all children of God. In one of Mother's talks, she told of my cousin Edna who had given herself to the lord by asking Him to come into her heart. It didn't quite add up if we belonged already, but if by asking we could make quite sure, I decided I too would like to belong and did the asking. I was then thirteen and when about a year later I wanted to be confirmed at the Free Church where we attended, I found I needed to be christened or baptised first. When I asked Mother why we had not been christened as babies, she said it was for us to decide when we were old enough to understand. I chose to be baptised as I had read in the Bible that complete immersion was correct. I went to the Baptist chapel in Ramsgate for this, as for some reason Mother didn't think the Broadstairs Chapel was appropriate. I still have the card with the October date 1933 that was given to me on that day. Not long after I was confirmed in the Free Church. Bishop Magee presided at the ceremony.

For a long time all the family had belonged to the Scripture Union. Mother was a branch secretary and gave out the cards. If one read the allotted scripture from the Bible each day, the whole Bible would be read in five years. In taking the cards round or the notes that some people had to go with them to local people for Mother, I used her bicycle and one day knocked over a little boy who had run straight out of his garden gate, between two hedges, into the road, so that I had not seen him coming. I dashed in after him when he ran back in crying, to apologise to his Mother, who said that he wasn't hurt and should not have run out of the gate. I certainly heaved a sigh of relief, and was careful not to ride so near the edge of the road in future. Quite a number of local people had the notes, which had to be given out every two months. Mother would mostly recruit people from the church. She was never backward in coming forward to introduce herself to any likely possible candidate for the Scripture Union. She also sometimes asked young people to her Sunday class and perhaps tea afterwards. One boy who came, who was I think in the choir, was Charlie Muir, elder brother to Frank Muir, who later became a household name. I am sure Charlie came to tea because he took a liking to me. I know he and I get on well in spite of the fact that I was extremely shy. I was teased about him and would go beetroot colour. It didn't last long. We had a sad farewell near the bottom gate of the kitchen garden, when he was going home for the last time, because his family was leaving Broadstairs to go to live in London. We had only known him a short time.

There were so many things that were quite different from where we had lived in the country at our other school. I missed seeing the glass show cases we had had. One had a stuffed heron in it that had lived by our pond. Another a badger and rabbits. I don't know what happened to those. There were other things like a cabinet of butterflies and bird's eggs, with names under them written in my father's beautiful neat writing. I had been in the habit of studying them, as the cabinet stood where I often passed and I could take my time looking at them. They seemed to have disappeared. There was plenty of compensation though. The main one was the beach or sands as we usually called them. Even in winter if it was a nice day we could go with the dogs to throw sticks for them. We didn't encourage Peggy or Bob if they were with us, to go in the sea, but there was always 'Chips' an old dark grey mongrel that probably did, but seemed to have no owner. He would be happy to fetch a stick for anyone who would throw one for him, from the sea or anywhere else.

There was another thing that was a bonus. We had some electric lights at boarding school, where we had also had some gaslights, that had a bypass to switch them on with, but we had only had lamps at home and never candles. To have electricity for lights and for power as well, was really good. We had electric irons and a floor cleaner that was used on the ground floors.

The church that we went to was very modern in comparison with the chapel we had mostly attended before. There were chairs instead of pews. There were ladies as well as men and boys in the choir. Dr Magee's eldest daughter, who had a good voice, sometimes sang a solo. After I had been confirmed I joined the youth club and was asked to be secretary. I had no idea what it might involve and was assured I would find it easy, as there were just a few notes to take and read out. I am afraid I soon found out it was not quite my scene and it wasn't long before I gave it up. After I had done a little teaching in the school at home, I was asked to teach in the Sunday School. I didn't imagine it would be very difficulty so readily agreed. However, I very soon found that the children who came to Sunday School, and who were mostly from the local school, were not like the children we had in our school. Some were far from disciplined, others not very bright. I just could not cope at that age and very soon gave that up too.

I did enjoy most of the church activities. One day Edith and I went together on a coach outing with others from the church. It was a Women's Meeting outing to which Mother was to have gone but for some reason she could not, so we went in her place. We took our cameras and our lunch with us and walked to the church where the coach was to start from. We left at about ten in the morning. There were about thirty on the coach. All were women except Dr Magee and one other man and the drive of course. I knew quite a number of the people. They were a friendly crowd. We went first to

Tenterden, the town near where I was born. The countryside we went through was very beautiful. Kent is not called 'The Garden of England' for nothing! We only spent half an hour there in order to stretch our legs. It had taken nearly two hours to get there. I am sure it would only take half that time these days. We went on through more beautiful countryside, taking a wrong turning at one point, to arrive at Crowbrough where we stopped to eat our lunch and get cups of tea. By then we were in East Sussex not far from Tunbridge Wells. As we came out from having our cups of tea, we saw what we thought was a very funny little man. He was only about three feet high and dressed in riding clothes. We all had a look in the church before moving on and Edith and I also looked in the stables nearby. We always like to see horses. We spent the next hour travelling to just beyond Maidstone where we went into the zoo. I was able to take a few photos. We then had a splendid tea of ham and salad and plenty of cakes. This was all arranged for our outing. We had more time to look at the animals afterwards. There were lions, deer, goats, bears, monkeys, birds, a camel and a hyena. There was one special run, where every animal was white. A cow, a pony, a goat, rabbits, guinea pigs, ducks and chickens. There were also some dingo pups, Australian wild dogs. Then there were foxes and wolves and a white parrot that danced if you told it to. There were five different kinds of bears. A polar bear sat up if you had something for it to eat. I fed a sloth bear with monkey nuts; it ate the shells too.

We had a short stop on the way home when I was able to pick a huge bunch of bluebells. As we arrived home we were singing, 'The day thou gavest Lord is ended'. We walked back from the church ready for our supper and bed feeling we had had a really good day out. I divided the bluebells I had picked and gave some to Mother taking the rest to an old lady I knew, who lived down the road.

There was a jumble sale on at the church hall one day where I was asked to help. Michael and another boy came to help me. I was told to look after the bookstall. The books were to be sold for one penny each. I spent a long time sorting the books out and arranging them before the doors were opened. When the doors were opened there was almost a stampede of people who went everywhere except to our stall. Hardly anyone wanted books. We took eleven pence! At the end, Dr Magee said we could have any we liked. We sorted a few and put them aside on the floor while we looked round the rest of the hall, before going home. When we came back for them, some of the ones we had chosen had been taken, but we took the remainder that we had put aside home with us. Although we didn't usually go to Sunday School, there was an occasion when it was to be conducted by the children themselves. Michael and I decided that we would go just to see what it was like, but I don't think we ever went again.

Besides the lady I took the bluebells to, there was a very old lady called Mrs Moses. The very name made me feel she was very old. The reason I knew her was because I was asked to sit with her a few times. I didn't really like to, as she seemed a bit odd. She was in bed all the time. She had a living in nurse to look after her. I don't know how Mother came to know her but when the nurse wanted to go somewhere with Mother, I sat by Mrs Moses and tried to make conversation. Sometimes what she said made sense and sometimes it didn't. She was quite harmless and in some ways I felt sorry for her but I was always apprehensive whenever I was there. Sometimes I read to her and once I showed her some photos. She showed me some Easter eggs and once gave me a banana. Because she lived in Ramsgate I was taken in Uncle Lewis' car and later fetched so I didn't have to go very often.

We had a visit from Uncle who came from Waters Land near where we used to live. When he visited us he asked if I would like to go out to tea with him. He said he was taking Mary too. Mary was the nursery nurse we had to look after us when we were small. Auntie and Uncle had brought her up. She was Auntie's stepsister. At that time she was matron in a school in Cliftonville where our previous assistant headmaster had by then, his own school. It was Uncle Lewis who took us to Margate and left the three of us to have a lovely tea. It was called a 'Devonshire Tea'. There were scones, cream, jam, cakes and tea. We had a job to eat it all, there was so much of it. We later walked along the prom, went into Woolworth's and made our way to the station where Uncle had to catch a train to go home. I had a go on a weighing machine, which said I was nine stone seven pounds. I was, of course, fully clothed, but I was rather pleased because not long before, my father had weighed me at home and although I knew I had grown a bit, I didn't think I had put on eighteen pounds in a few months to make my weight over ten stone, which is what his scales told us. I rather think the scales at the station were more correct, at least I like to think so. It wasn't long before Uncle Lewis came along to pick us up and leave Uncle to catch his train. Uncle Lewis took Mary back to her school first and then took me home.

There were other times when some of us would go out in a crowd to either Dreamland, the fun fare in Margate or Merrie England in Ramsgate. These trips were few and far between as I, for one, never had any money for such luxury. There was one occasion when I managed to get half-a-crown from my father when we were going to Merrie England. This was unheard of, so much so that I can 'see' him now, giving it to me. I was for a change, able to go on the 'ghost train' and a few of the other amusements.

When we went hiking as we sometimes did, we often sang as we marched along. The then new one, 'I'm happy when I'm hiking', or some of the ones from the first World War like 'Ta-ra-ra-boomdiay' and then there was, 'There ain't no sense sitting on the fence, all by yourself in the moonlight', and a few others. The best time to sing them was when we were out in the country where we couldn't be heard by those who disapproved.

Walking along in the town one could often see a 'stop me and buy one'. This was a man on a tricycle with a large insulated box packed with ice, in the front. He rang his bell as he rode along. If you put your hand up to him he would stop for you to buy an ice cream of some kind from him. With, as usual, very little money, I rarely stopped him. My pocket money didn't run to such things as ice cream. It was possible to buy a snow fruit. It cost one penny, was about five inches in length, triangular shaped and consisted of frozen flavoured water. There were various fruit flavours, which were lovely on a hot day. Handed to you wrapped in a thin piece of card, which could be torn off, it soon melted and trickled down your hand. However, the joy of the taste far outweighed the nuisance of the mess. There was a lady called Mrs Bennett who was a friend of Mother's. She ran a boarding house like many other people in Broadstairs, but she had a special hobby, which was making delicious homemade sweets. It was her sweets that I carried on a tray at the fete to sell. I was sometimes sent to buy sweets from her rather than buy them in the shops. Her fudge was excellent but she had a variety of other sweets. I know she ran her boarding house for many years because I have seen it advertised over the years. I often wondered how long she kept her hobby going!

A new Ice Cream Parlour was opened while we were at Broadstairs. It hadn't been there long when some of us went there. I was treated to a 'Knickerbocker glory'. It was huge and luscious and of course I ate it all. I was then offered a glass of hot Horlicks, being the 'piggy' that I was I couldn't resist it and soon after I'd finished it, returned the lot! That taught me a lesson. I was not used to doing that at all! I obviously wasn't used to such rich food. A Mars bar was about the extent of my consumption of sweets. We always had four good meals a day so I had no real need to eat in between, but just occasionally a bar of Mackintoshes toffee was rather nice to suck, it would last longer than a Mars bar! The toffee only cost one penny, the Mars bar two pence.

From the age of fourteen to sixteen I kept a detailed account of every halfpenny I received or spent, in a notebook. Although I had regular pocket money, at first sixpence (old pence of course) each week, I fairly often had handouts from visiting relations or friends. This could be anything from sixpence to half-a-crown. Grandpa often gave me sixpence. I needed some pyjamas at one time so asked my father for the six shillings that was needed to buy them and he gave it to me. I had mostly boys pyjamas passed on to me before. The cost was in fact five shillings and eleven pence half penny. This left me with a spare halfpenny. I could and did buy sugar with which to feed the horses for a halfpenny. Edith and I by then, often went to look at and feed the horses in the stables not far out of the town, if we had anything for them. When I wanted or should I say needed shoes, I asked for four shillings and was able to buy sandals, which lasted all the summer for three shillings and eleven pence half penny. That spare halfpenny went on sweets! The priority item from my pocket money was a penny for church. Two pennies if I went to church in the evening as well as the morning. Other purchases were for birthday presents. They could cost from a penny to a shilling or more, depending on whose birthday it was. I often bought a skein of wool for four pence halfpenny. Then I had to wind it into a ball myself. One column in my note book reads, candles a penny half penny, blotting paper, which we were always having to use as the ink on a pen never dried very quickly and there was no such thing as a biro or ballpoint, one and a half pence, envelopes two pence, lemon one penny, gave Michael a half penny and so on! As time went on I had eight pence pocket money. Wool was six pence, Lux was two pence, and matches a penny. At Christmas time I had extra money given to me as presents from various relations but I had a very large number of present to buy, which ranged from a pencil for a penny to a dictionary for someone for six pence, and more for a few other things.

After my birthday when I was given even more money, I managed to put three shillings and six pence into my Post Office savings book. This I had had since I was seven and we all had forms to put penny stamps on. When we had eleven stamps on Mother would add one more to make one shilling. This could then be put into the savings book. One could not put less at any one time. My father gave me two shillings for stockings when I asked him. I paid only one shilling and seven pence for them. That left me with a bonus. I bought a purse for three pence for my dearly beloved boyfriend Roy. It must have been his birthday! Then pocket money went up to one shilling eventually. I bought material to make myself a cotton petticoat. This cost two shillings and two pence half penny. I managed at one time to get ten shillings from my father for shoes that cost six shillings and eleven pence, and stockings that were only one shilling. My father never expected any change so I did well out of that. I spent three pence on a torch battery and one penny on a packet of 'Imps'. They were a kind of lozenge for sucking when one had a sore throat. A film for my box camera cost one shilling. I took as many photographs as I could afford to. By then we had eight negatives on a roll where there had previously been only six. Toothpaste was sixpence, tooth powder only three pence so I usually bought the powder. When Edith and I went on the coach outing to the zoo I paid three shillings for it. I was just fifteen then and had not started to have wages rather than pocket money, which was three shillings per week when it started about six months later. I had had a little more for my birthday but I couldn't ask for money for clothes or shoes once I had wages, and I bought a hat for two shillings. There were many others things I spent my money on in those two years, to numerous to mention but in the end I had received one way or another, twelve pounds, twelve shillings and eight pence half penny. I had spent ten pounds fourteen shillings and nine pence. Some of it was saved in my Post Office savings book and I had nearly two pounds left. I have little record of what I did with that or any future monies. I didn't feel hard done by and I learned to be thrifty, which was to my advantage in later life when times were hard. My father was not as mean as it may sound. In fact he was really very generous. Because of his generosity many school fees were waived or just not paid, so he was quite hard up at times. I knew nothing of this until much later. I liked to be generous so a lot of my money was stretched to as many presents as I could possibly make it.

There were many people with whom I had plenty of contact during those years. Some, more than others, as well as my own family. People who, on a temporary basis lived with us. Toots was one of these people. She had stayed with us when I was younger and I had stayed at her home in Folkestone. Her family moved to Kingsnorth, near Ashford where I went to stay. My father gave me the money for the train fare. At their home they had Judy the dog and Punch a nice little cat, but not to be compared, in my eyes, with the very handsome Toodles that belonged to Uncle at Water's Land, that had lived to be over seventeen years. While staying with Toots we went to baby-sit for neighbours of theirs. I thought it quite extraordinary that the nearly two year old child we were sitting in with, was asleep in a pram in the same room as we were, the whole of the evening. I could not understand why it was not in a cot upstairs. I was also surprised that we could talk and have what we called at that time, the wireless on, all evening without the child waking. Toots was a couple of years older than I. She came to us at Broadstairs to help look after some of the boys in the holidays. There were always plenty there. She didn't stay very long because, she told me many years later, it didn't work out very well.

My second cousin Beryl, who was about ten years older than I, was with us for some while. She was really great to be with and to chat to. I could confide in her on any subject, better than I could my sisters. Beryl called Mother Auntie Grace but Mother often didn't approve of the way Beryl conducted her life. I think Mother found her a bit flamboyant, though she would agree that she worked well at anything she undertook. We quite often went on the sands with her little one Fayza in the pram to enjoy an afternoon and sometimes there would be one or two others with us. If there were several of us we rather liked to go further along away from the main bay where it was quieter, if a bit rocky where baby crabs could be found. There were of course many walks with the dogs on the sands. Winifred or Irene Budding sometimes came, or we might have some boys with us. There was one afternoon when I took three of the boys aged about eight to the sands. One of them had a large sailing yacht and they played by the water. This was in the holidays. I was sitting on the steps knitting and eating a Mars bar, when I realised they had all got their socks wet I made them come up on the dry sand away from the water. Later when we went home for tea they had to change into clean dry socks. Sometimes I took quite a number of the younger boys for a walk right out into the country where we could see the horses at the stables and ducks and chickens and other farm animals on a farm nearby, then back near the sea where the band was sometimes playing on the bandstand.

Roy had two sisters. They both visited on one or two occasions. Joyce the older one came to stay. Not long enough for me to get to know her well. She seemed a very nice girl. Later she went on to study medicine like most of her family, including her father who was a doctor in the West Indies. Roy broke his leg one day. Because he played cricket rather well and was older than most of the boys in the school he was in the habit of going to play with a local team in the evening. He came out to the road after playing just as a car was coming. He leapt into the air, he was a good jumper too, attempting to avoid the car and landed on the bonnet, then rolled off. I never was quite sure if a wheel went over his leg or not. He didn't seem to know himself, however his leg was broken and he went to a private ward in Ramsgate Hospital. While he was there Mother let me go with her when she visited him. I think my sister Dorothea came once and I know Edith did more than once. It wasn't much fun being in the ward with Mother there, but it was better than not being there. When we all started off down the corridor to go home, I had managed to leave gloves behind, or suddenly thought of something I had forgotten to ask, so dashed back to retrieve the gloves in order to steal a much longed for kiss!

When he came out of hospital, Roy was put in a dormitory that had somewhat younger boys than he was usually with because it was on a lower floor. It was easier for him with crutches not to have to go to the top floor where he would normally be, and as he had to take it easy at first, he had breakfast in bed and could then take his time getting up. I usually took his breakfast up and made up for lost time on the kisses I had missed. Sometimes Edith or Betty were asked to take something up to him, though I tried to get there first if I could. When he was well enough to travel, at the end of the term, he went away to stay with his uncle for some weeks. The day after he had gone, Edith wasn't so well so Betty was about to take a cup of tea to her, when Mother asked her to take one to Roy at the same time. She had to stop mid sentence when she remembered he was not there. I had been used to clearing Roy's breakfast tray away, generally clearing up after him and making his bed. I found it most distressing not to have any of that to do as I enjoyed doing it.

We were not able to write to each other as the post would have been seen, and that was not allowed, so all the time he was gone, he had no news of me or I of him, except about twice or three times. The first time was when he sent a postcard to Mother. It was breakfast time. She had shown it to Winifred and Edith. Then I came into the room and spotted it, so she showed it to me then passed it to Mr White, a master at that time. Mr White remarked on the last message where he had sent love to everyone, so Winifred promptly said, "That message was for no one but Brenda!"

There was a special CSSM meeting in Westminster Central Hall to which Mother was going and said I could go too. We went by train arriving in London by eleven thirty. As Dorothea was ill in the hospital at Hackney where she was training we went to see her first. Sylvia had been there, doing her nursing training for some time so we were able to see her too. As Dorothea was in bed I had dinner with her. At half past one we left to go to the Central Mall where we knew that Roy and his uncle would be. Roy's uncle was a keen Christian as Mother was, so they got on like a house on fire so to speak! We spent some time looking for them and found them just as the meeting was about to start. We had tea in between the two meetings and I was thrilled to bits to see Roy. I just longed to fling my arms round him and hug and kiss him but I couldn't even touch him. However, it was lovely to have a chat, but poor Roy looked so sad when we finally had to leave, after the evening meeting to walk along to get the train. It was midnight by the time we were home. I had bought a Mars bar with the intention of eating it but having to leave Roy meant I just wasn't hungry. He was still using crutches so I didn't know how long it would be before I saw him again. In the event it was nearly another four weeks when I heard Mother telling some of the boys that he was walking without crutches or stick. I was over the moon and Roy came back a few days later. By then it was term time again and many things had happened. While Roy was away I had been doing a lot of helping one way and another. I was still as it were a schoolgirl trying to cope with lessons and study. At some point after we had all moved over to the school, Irene Budding who was matron, moved out to a house of her own and later worked in a large children's home on the east cliff. Mother took on matron's duties helped by various others and me. However, Irene whom we all still called Miss Budding, or nick named behind her back, 'M'me Pud', was a frequent visitor, coming mainly to see my father of whom she was particularly fond. She could walk in as and when she liked. The front door was unlocked all day. Some of us visited her in her home. Betty and I went to sit with two of the boys who had come back from the isolation hospital. They went to stay with her before returning to the school. We went together or in turn when Miss Budding wanted to go out. My father sent me with messages to her sometimes. She had Peggy, her dog there, so I went to take Peggy out for a walk, or to go walking with Miss Budding and Peggy. When Peggy had puppies I was very pleased to go and see them. One Easter I went with Miss Budding to the Good Friday service at the Church of England where she attended, to see what it was like. It lasted three hours, I didn't enjoy that very much.

The whole of the time that Roy was away I wrote in two exercise books everything I had been doing each day for him to read on his return. The first one has forty-five pages and the second; a rather smaller one has thirty-two pages. Although I gave them to him to read, I wouldn't let him keep them in case he left them anywhere for someone to pick up and I still have those books. They are a very nostalgic source of information to me.

I had forgotten that Edith played the piano. I often sat reading while listening to her playing. I knew I often tried to, and even managed on a few occasions when there was no one else who could, to play the hymns for school prayers. I had never really had lessons except for a few from Mother when I was about eight, because I was so keen to learn, so it had to be mainly self taught. I was able to find a very few hymns with no sharps or flats or may be just one of either, and in this way got by. We also played records on a wind up gramophone quite often. We had to be careful not to play just after dinner as that was when Mother had her rest and the gramophone was in what was by then a common room, used by staff and sometimes, senior boys or girls. It was immediately beneath Mother's bedroom. We had one record, which was a song sung in German. As we were learning German we thought it good to sing it and sang it often.

Particularly during the holidays we not only went in the common room at times but inhabited the drawing room and library if they were free when we liked. Edith was nearly always with me though she and her brother Brian went for a short while to stay with their Gran while their parents were in China. When they had not been with us very long, their Gran came to visit. She was taken into the Japanese garden and somehow slipped on the stepping stones that were the only means of crossing the stream. Brian who was only seven at the time, reported afterwards that, "Gran got ducked in the pond!" We all thought his quote was a huge laugh.

I frequently had to go to the dentist and had filling after filling. I didn't mind much, I got used to it. I sometimes took one of the boys with me. They usually had to have just a check up. Winifred was away for a time so I wrote letters to her and sometimes typed them on the enormous typewriter that we had. I wrote regularly to the others, Sylvia, Dorothea and Peter when they were not at home as well as writing to Edith when she was away and other friends and relations. There was a boy by the name of Gordon who was friendly with Michael. They often went out cycling together. Edith and I were at the stables one-day when they came along on their bicycles. After we had been there some time helping, which we did at times, Edith 'bagged' Gordon's bicycle and went home with Michael, so Gordon and I had to walk home together. There were two girls called Betty, both had younger brothers in the school. Betty Jeffreys also had a sister Jane who had long flowing very fair hair. Their younger brother David also had very fair hair and usually a very high colour. He was one of the boys who had scarlet fever. The other Betty who was older lived locally, her brother was a weekly boarder, who was younger. Betty was a little older than I and stayed at home some of the time. When she was with us she did quite a lot of the helping, with me. We often made the boys beds together. Edith didn't do much helping, but even she did some of the ironing.

Reg Hitch didn't drive but had the use of a hired car and driver when he liked. When Monsieur Pithard was going home for the holidays Reg took him to Dover. We were invited to go too. Edith was very keen as she liked Reg, and Betty was pleased to join in the fun. I was not at all keen as I was not at that time particularly fond of Reg, he always seemed to me to make not very kind sarcastic remarks, but the others persuaded me. Dover was not too far and it was quite a pleasant trip.

Peter came home for the Easter weekend. Michael, Gordon and I met him at the station. Peter's bedroom was called 'The Admiralty'. While he was at home we acquired food for a feast. In the afternoon we all went for a picnic. Some of the boys who were there for the holidays, Peter, Michael, Betty, Edith and I all went. We were home by half past seven. I as usual saw the boys to bed, while the others played 'murder', a favourite game at that time! Then Peter, Betty,

Edith and I had our feast in 'The Admiralty'. Two fried eggs each with bacon and potato, a huge plateful of pineapple and cream, followed by coffee. There were biscuits too but we couldn't manage all of them so we took the remainder and some cream down to Mother in her bedroom.

I was forever dusting and tidying various places. Particularly the drawing room on a Sunday before going to church, in case visitors came. There were times when Uncle Lewis would take some of us out in his car, often at Mother's request when she wanted to visit a friend. There were other times when some of us had informal chats with my father, during which time he would sometimes fall asleep. Big as I was, I sometimes sat on his knew which I enjoyed, and he seemed quite happy with. Mother and my father had very little to do with each other. They were rarely seen in the same room together. They never openly argued or fell out in any way as far as I know. I would light the fire for my father, help sort books or do other little jobs for him and was very happy to do so. I painted a chest of draws in one of the dormitories one day which made me late for dinner. In fact I arrived in the dining room when everyone else had finished. However, I had mine cold, but I didn't mind and as it was holidays neither did anyone. I picked primroses and violets in the Jap garden as we called it, and found a vase to put them in to give to my father.

I went out to buy fruit for some of the boys. There was a special arrangement for boys to have their own fruit, which we got for them but it went on the account for their parents to pay. I wonder now how much of that was paid for. I didn't have to take money to get it as I asked for it to be put on the school account at the shop. After tea the fruit was given out to the boys who were to have it. One of the many things I usually did. I used to feel sorry for the boys who didn't have any because their parents hadn't ordered it.

My father showed me some mustard and cress he had sown on blotting paper, one day, obviously rather pleased that it had grown. It was not the sort of thing he did as a rule.

I spent some time mending. There were always things that needed mending. Mother did most of it for the boys. Mother sometimes had family prayers in her room in the evening if any of the others were home, during the holidays, because there was no school prayers for the boys that stayed on through most the holidays which quite a number did.

One very small boy called Hector had a Mother who was a doctor but he had no father. He was very bright but still not quite six when he first came. He had been looked after by a nanny who had done everything for him. He couldn't even dress himself. He was a nice child and sometimes quite unintentionally a real comic. On occasion if thwarted he would create in some way. I once found all his bedclothes on the floor because he had not got, and could not find his clothes. He was sent into another dormitory on his own to cool off.

Some boys went home and returned to school at any time to suit their families, during the holidays, so numbers varied. I mostly had the job of getting their things packed ready to go or unpacked and put away when they returned. We had a lot of foreign students in the school. Most of them were French, though not all. I had the job of welcoming them as I could speak French. However, as I showed them where various things were and explained things to them I had to bear in mind that they had come to learn English. Each sentence was therefore said first in English, then in French and then often in English again. With a final question of, "Do you understand"? It was not so easy if students were German or Spanish or from some other country.

One holiday we had about twenty French girls all at once. They had most of the dormitories to sleep in between them while the usual occupants slept out in tents. They were with us for two weeks. I was truly thankful when they left. They were the most untidy crowd I've ever met. We gave them waste paper baskets but they filled them to overflowing with all kinds of rubbish and heaps of dirty cotton wool, in spite of having them emptied daily. Fortunately we had very little to do with them, except to clear up after them, because they were out all day from after breakfast and again after an early evening meal, so we hardly saw them. They had their own leader in charge of them, and I felt it was just as well it was only the once and for only two weeks. We had a lot of boys for short or long periods. One boy was thirteen when he came. He knew no English at first but soon learned and fitted into school lessons in no time quite well. He was with us for two or three years and was very popular. Another older boy of about seventeen was with us for most of a year. He was very keen to learn English. He asked me one day to give him a dictation. I was a little reluctant to do so, as he was a bit cheeky at times, pulling my hair and such like. However, carefully keeping my distance I agreed to do as he had asked and at the end hastily made an excuse to leave him to do his own corrections from the book. When I saw him later I asked him how many mistakes he had made to which he replied, "about four or five". He was one of a number of boys who was obviously quite keen on me, and although quite flattered, I didn't really want to know. In any case I had to be careful as Roy easily became very jealous. I have a number of autographs in my book which include not only the French boy but other admirers and also many other friends and members of the family including Mother and my father and last but not least my beloved Roy and another Roy who was the one I fancied when I was only eight and he was about six months younger.

Plate Titles

Section Three

17) 1934. Me with Roy's sister Joyce in the Japanese garden.

18) Me wearing 'modesty vest'.

19) Me with Dennis Storey on the sands.

20) Me knitting in the Winter Garden.

21) Winifred with the dogs on the sands.

22) 1934. The College.

23) 1934. A lion in the zoo near maidstone.

CHAPTER V

MY FATHER WAS ILL

1934 was a very memorable year. I was fifteen in February. I have already told of some things but there are many more. During the Easter holidays while Roy was away I was never lost for something to do, but still found time to write almost every day. After painting the chest of draws, I painted the landing, the stairs and then a classroom, another day. I had watched Walter painting the dormitories so was well versed in how to cope, and enjoyed doing it.

Edith and I were sleeping in the bunk bedroom. Uncle Lewis had built the bunks so that two people could comfortable sleep in the one room. We found one day that we had bites on us in quite large numbers, when the weather became warm and then some peculiar marks on our sheets. Investigation was made and it was discovered that behind the wallpaper, which had been put on top of a very open canvas, that was stretched across a wooden frame, were house bugs. Ugh! It was said they must have been dormant for some time but no one could throw any light on as to how long they had been there, or why they had surfaced. It was suggested that the warm weather had something to do with it. We moved to a room across the landing. We emptied everything from the room. We then stripped layers and layers of paper from the walls, exposing the canvas. After much fumigation we then repapered the walls. First with a plain paper and then with a blue patterned one. Uncle Lewis helped us. It was quite an experience. A number of people came to have a look while we were taking the paper off when they heard about the canvas underneath. Michael often popped in to have a look and my father came to see what we were up to and to advise us.

Edith was away part of the time and on her return as Peter was back on his training ship, Edith used his room, 'The Admiralty' for a while. I was in what had been a dormitory for the very youngest boys. As it was holidays only Georgie, the youngest of the three Wall boys was in there, so I had him in with me. It was a lovely room overlooking the lily pond and the allotments beyond. I had the head of my bed right in the middle of the large square bay window. Most mornings were sunny but when it rained it came in the window if I'd left it open. As the mornings grew lighter and I nearly always woke early, I had all the light I could possibly need in the morning to see to read or even write sometimes. I usually read the Scripture Union portion from the Bible and then whatever book I had on the go. Georgie was a very sweet little boy. He had a lovely singing voice. Sometimes when he woke he would lie in bed singing to himself, which I enjoyed listening to. Sometimes he sang hymns, sometimes songs. If he was awake when I wanted to get up I put on a dressing gown and took my clothes down to the bathroom to dress after my bath. At night he was asleep when I went to bed and the light didn't wake him, so again I could read. I was an avid reader, if a slow one and had access to many books. I did sometimes read during the day, maybe sitting on the lawn, particularly if the book I had was compulsive reading and I had a job to put it down, but there was not often time for day time reading, there were so many other things to do. Just as we had done a lot of moving around of rooms at our previous school so we did at this one. Although we moved back into the newly papered bunk room, it soon became occupied by others. I think at that time it may have been my cousin Beryl with her small daughter Fayza. Edith and I with Betty then had the other bedroom and Georgie and others who had used it as a dormitory were moved into another dormitory. At one time Peter had occupied the very small bedroom between Mother's room and dormitory one, before he had the one called 'The Admiralty' on the next floor up, when he was at home. Then Uncle Lewis had the very small bedroom. 'The Admiralty' which was between the bunk room and the bedroom we moved to, was temporarily used by Edith because I had Georgie in with me, but suddenly it was all changed. One day my father was looking, 'not very well' when Sylvia was home on a short break. This was literally quite unknown at any time before, by me, or, Mother told by her, in all the thirty-five years, or thereabouts that she had known him. Sylvia said she thought he had a temperature, so he let her take it. It was too high to be left untreated and he was taken up to 'The Admiralty' to bed. It was quieter that end of the house and he wouldn't have all his office papers around him to look at. I was sent to find a doctor. The first was not available but the second one came. Mother then told us that my father might have to go into hospital. However, in the event he didn't go but from then on for the rest of his life he was very careful about his diet. It was just as well Sylvia had been at home, as I can't imagine anyone else being able to persuade him hat he was ill, let along that he needed the attention of a doctor. He didn't know what it was to be ill. It was never confirmed, as he had no x-ray, but it was suggested that he had gallstones. He made a fairly good recovery in a reasonable time, but at the time he gave great concern to a large number of people.

Not long before this episode Dorothea who had been at Hackney Hospital for I think, only about six months or less, training as a nurse, had rheumatic fever and had to be discharged. She was at home convalescing and spent much time sleeping in order to recoup. Sylvia who came home after a stint on night duty also slept by day at times, so it was not unusual to find both of them asleep on occasions.

When Sylvia came home one time, she gave me a tin of toffees and Michael something similar. I gave some to the younger boys whom I usually supervised getting up or going to bed. One day I threw toffees into the dormitory and shouted "scrambles". One boy picked up four, another one two. It was in the morning. I told them not to eat them before breakfast. What a hope! They had all been eaten by the time they sat down to breakfast. Georgie was in a dormitory on his own at the time so I gave him some separately. Some of the others were unlucky with the scrambles. One of them was very cheeky so I sent him to my father who gave him a lecture.

There were times when boys were out of bed in the evening when they should not have been and sometimes I sent them to him and they received a taste of the slipper! Poor kids! But that is what was not only quite usual by way of punishment but also quite acceptable. There were other things that were accepted then, that are unheard of these days. Betty and I went to the swimming baths in Margate, there were none in Broadstairs, at a time when it was mixed bathing. There were other sessions for men only or women only. We went only rarely and didn't think twice about the fact that it was mixed bathing, but many people didn't like that.

I had to wear what was known as a modesty vest in the front of my dress. It was my best for Sunday dress and could not be washed, only dry cleaned, which was expensive, so a small piece of material that looked nice was pinned underneath to go across the V neck of the dress and could be washed and changed as and when necessary.

We had electric light switches made of metal. They were round with a small knob, which was the actual switch, in the middle. They are not used these days. We learned that it was essential to remember, never to tough one with a wet hand, because it was dangerous, we might receive an electric shock. I tied a string round the switch in my bedroom and fixed it in such a way that if I pulled it I could put it out from my bed. Not very safe, but I thought it was ingenious, not dangerous!

The boys had hair grease as often as not to keep the hair on the top of their heads flat, neat and tidy. One of the most popular types of hair grease was a small oval tin of Field's lavender brilliantine. It could be bought from Woolworth's for only a few pence, the few pence being one reason for its popularity.

We did have another cat, I don't remember exactly when or for how long. He was a super cat so was named 'Super' but I don't seem to have a photo of him and wonder what happened to him. I used my camera as often as funds would permit and sometimes persuaded others to use it so that I could be on my film. It was a very easy to use Kodak Brownie box camera, which I had saved up for and bought when I was ten years old. I was able to buy it at half price as it came from my Uncle Edwin's chemist shop.

When we went for walks we sometimes picked green food for Noel, Dorothea's rabbit, and at other times in the garden if there was any to be had. Noel was still with us at first but later went to be looked after by Auntie at Water's Lane when Dorothea left home.

The gramophone we had was portable. It had a handle to wind it up for each record we put on and had or at least was supposed to have a new needle for every record. I don't think it did have though, as we knew each needle would play more than one record, though it didn't do the record any good. In the summer we took it out on the lawn, which was all right if we turned it so that the lid shaded the sun from the actual record. We had what we thought were good modern tunes of all kinds, including a German love song which we rather liked and sang in German, with it. We were not meant to play jazz but we sometimes did.

There were a lot of places with boys names on, like lockers and shelves in the bathroom and wash room, on labels, and where coats were kept and such like. From time to time as boys left, or new boys came, these had to be changed, so I found myself scrubbing at labels to remove them and putting new ones in all kinds of places. Another thing that had to be done was cleaning out inkwells if they had bits in them other than ink, and then refilling them and topping up any that needed it. Blotting paper was one of the things often to be found and of course, the odd fly or wasp.

There was one French boy who was older than most. We had little to do with him. He was a fairly quiet studious boy who was not with us very long but he spent a lot of time drawing, which he did well. He liked doing portraits and did quite a number. He persuaded me to 'sit' for him to draw a portrait of me. I was reluctant at first. He just did little more than head and shoulders as I was, and made a very good job of it. As I write I can't find it though I know I kept it a long time. It might just turn up. Who knows! There was another boy who was a German student. He was nineteen. He played the piano well mostly from ear. A lot of it was jazz, and a lot of us used to badger him to give us a tune, we did so enjoy hearing and watching him. Mostly he would oblige. There was nothing musically, that I liked better than to hear the piano played well.

We had various visitors who just turned up at times. One day it was Mrs Campbell and her second son Frank. There had been four Campbell boys at our previous school all at the same time and my parents had known the family for many years. They had by then left, but had come to see my parents and to see what the new school was like. We were in the library doing prep and had to move out as my father decided to entertain them in the library and Mother came down to see them too. I t was not unusual for 'old boys' to visit us. It happened all the time.

When Mother and I were out one-day, Bishop Magee's wife and son Arthur, who was driving, came along. They stopped and gave us a lift in their car. Arthur was not often at home so we didn't get to know him very well. We knew his sisters, particularly the younger one who was about the same age as Dorothea.

They had a badminton court at the church hall and as I had played when I was away at school, I thought I would go and join in a game. It cost three pence to attend a session. Unfortunately I found the players too good for me so I only went once.

Edith and I went to a Red Cross exhibition. We were given free samples of Ovaltine, not something we usually had, but we certainly enjoyed it when we got home.

There was a master who was only with us a short time. He was far from popular either with pupils or staff. He was washing his hands at the bathroom basin one day, which was near the door, which was wide open. I came along and made some very innocent remark, and evidently smiled as I did so. For some reason he thought I was mocking him and slapped my face accusing me of 'grinning' at him. I went straight up to my father to tell him what had happened. That master didn't last another day and no one was sorry to see him go.

When my father was ill, Winifred took over a number of duties he would normally have done. One was to read the boys' Sunday letters that had to go to their parents. I helped by putting them in the envelopes, licking and sticking them up and putting the stamps on. I liked the taste of the glue!

There was one boy I spent some while with, though I don't remember his name. He was only slightly older than I and was only with us during the summer holidays, not during the term time. We would lie on separate beds in an open tent with our Bibles. For some reason we both liked to read, discuss, and argue quite amicably, over various passages. It must have been another time when Roy had gone to stay with his uncle, as he would have created if he had known about it, but I never could see why one shouldn't have a boy for a friend, without him being ones' boyfriend!

Three of us in the family from time to time had stys in our eyes. Sylvia had suffered a lot and had been given malt and cod liver oil and beemax to improve her health, which must have worked, as she grew out of them. I was nine years old the last time I had three at once, two on one eye and one on the other but I wasn't given anything to help improve my health. I just had to rest! However, I did grow out of them after that. Michael had them and felt quite under the weather. With one of his eyes bandaged I helped him to get to bed and administered to him, taking bread and milk to him in bed. A favourite dish! My father said he had them as a child and like us, he grew out of having them.

Mother was very keen on general knowledge. In order to help when my father was ill she had the whole school together to give them a general knowledge lesson. It usually took the form of all kinds of questions to see how many could be answered and then going through them telling everyone the correct answers, explaining about them as she went along. She could be very strict and was a firm but fair disciplinarian, giving praise where it was due. She had no trouble handling so many at once.

Miss Budding came quite often to see how my father was when he was ill, and when he was getting better. Although she had left, I think she still felt as if she belonged, she had been with us so long. She helped by having two of the boys at her home when they came back from hospital. Betty and I went to sit with them and to see them. We also went to her home to help with Peggy's puppies. Miss Budding brought them to the school one day for my father to see them, but she must have found homes for all of them, as she didn't keep any.

I walked down the garden to go into the town one day while Roy was still away. I found Walter digging the kitchen garden. He was a really good sort and did all kinds of things. He stopped to ask me about when I had been up to London for the day and asked me how Roy was getting on. As he was just finishing and going home I walked down the road with him and told him about Roy and about the whole day.

When I found I had to do more and yet more chores, I had little time for schoolwork. Times in the thirties were hard for most people. We had always understood that there was very little money to spare but beyond that finances in general were not discussed. I was certainly told nothing. Mother used to say, "People think that because we live in a large house, we have plenty of money, but they just don't know or understand that we haven't".

A person, who came in daily to clean dormitories and bathrooms through the week, left. We had previously had various people. One was a peculiar little person, who also did our room. She managed to knock the top off a glass powder bowl of mine and break it. I was very upset at the time. I still have the bowl with the powder puff, which is attached to a handkerchief, in it, and some powder. I can't think why I've kept it. I haven't used it for years, and I don't remember who gave it to me! Miss Budding had at one time, when we couldn't get anyone else, seen to some of the cleaning and enlisted our help on Saturdays to clean and polish all the stairs and landings, but that was before she left. Sometimes it fell to my lot to do all these things, with almost no time for anything else. That left just Emily, Walter and Jesse who were staunch and loyal servants to the end. I told Mother one day that if I had to do so much cleaning each morning I did not have time for lessons. "Well, I'm afraid you will have to forget the lessons," she said. I didn't really mind very much at first.

As the summer went on that year the boys played cricket against other schools in the town. We had no sports field belonging to the school. PE could be done on the lawn, but a field up the road had to be used otherwise. There was Stonehouse School, which became Bradstow College. There were many others but names escape me except Richmond House School where our boys once won against them. The score was twenty-seven to nine. I don't remember them playing against Chatham House which was the Grammar School in Ramsgate where the Prime Minister Edward Heath went as a boy, and where some boys took their lunch to eat at midday at school. Our few dayboys went home for their midday meal.

I often put the sports clothes out for the boys and helped the younger ones to get into theirs.

Michael was still at home for the summer but later in September he went to St Lawrence College, a public school at the back of Ramsgate, as a dayboy. He cycled each way and grew fast. He was only there about two years and was ill part of that time because he outgrew his strength. It was an easy fairly flat ride of about two or three miles each way. Of course at that time everyone had to have a bell on their bicycles and they were much heavier machines than those used today. Just a few times we walked to St Lawrence College on Sunday evening to attend the College Chapel, which was open to anyone, but it was quite a walk so we didn't go many times.

During the summer we often spent time in the Jap Garden, as we called it. Edith took a photo of me with my camera and I took one of her with hers. Then when Roy's sister, Joyce was with us we had a session of taking photos. Joyce used my camera to take one of me with Roy. I don't seem to have one of his younger sister, Avice, though.

There are quite a few boys that I don't recall though in some cases I know their names.

My cousin John who came from Wales was with us for a short time. My Uncle who was my father's brother decided he needed some coaching, to get him through his exams. He was a year older than I was.

On the sands there were talent shows with Uncle Mack where children won prizes and sandcastle competitions too for children to win prizes. We didn't join in with those, though sometimes we saw them. There was the annual water sports which was good to watch but again we didn't enter anything. There was a paddle steamer that went from Margate to London but we didn't go on that.

A safety boat was out in the bay during the season in the daytime, and a raft that one could swim out to and climb on, then if it was deep enough one could dive from it. I went on it a few times but I didn't dive. Others dived from the jetty too. No one was allowed to go beyond the safety boat when swimming. If they tried, the man in the boat soon shouted at them. When the sea was too rough to be safe to swim there was no safety boat but a red warning flag was put up to stop people going in for a swim.

My exercise books that I still have tell me that I finished my schooling eventually in July 1934, and I hadn't been doing very regular lessons for some while. My English book has 'Sir Galahad' on the first page. In it, it has, not only English but Literature, Grammar, composition, Repetition, Diction, Spelling with nearly as many crosses as ticks, History, Geography, Scripture and General Knowledge. There are lovely very colourful maps of England, Europe, USA, Africa, Australia and others. I really enjoyed Geography. I wonder if I inherited the love of Geography from my father. He had a Geographical degree amongst others. He may have passed on the inability to spell too as he told me that he always had to have a dictionary handy in his study. My spelling shows numerous mistakes on many pages but we rarely had marks as such, so I don't know how good I was at the other subjects, except for Maths. Unfortunately I don't have a Maths book of that era. What a pity because I know that I was good at that and enjoyed it. I only have an Arithmetic book dated January to May 1928 when I was nine. I have far more ticks than crosses against the long multiplication and long division of decimals that I did during that time. I also have a writing book dated January to May 1925. I was then just six and it is in what we called long hand but is now called joined writing. I wasn't even in school with the boys then. Some of it is in ink, that meant that I used a pen with a nib that had to be dipped into an inkwell, and the ink didn't dry very quickly, so smudged easily if there was no blotting paper to dry it. The only other 1934 exercise book I have is a German book. I learned for nearly two years. It is all in German script and I can't now read more than a very few words of it. I remember that it was Reg Hitch who taught us. His German was perfect. During the war he was in intelligence because of that. Anyone could have taught us in the other subjects but mostly it was Winifred.

As I said, I didn't mind much at first and was eventually given three pounds per week as wages and expected to meet my own expenses. Roy was still with us for a time but then he left. He had been with us for three years and he was nineteen. For nearly a year I became assistant matron cum cleaner. I continued to supervise the younger boys going to bed, and bathing the very youngest, and getting them up in the morning. We had one unfortunate boy who was nine. He wet his bed almost without fail every night in spite of being hauled out of bed very late after he had gone to sleep, as often as not by me, in order to perform, but it didn't help much. He had to put his sheet in the bath in the morning and I usually rinsed it out and hung it on the line. I gave out any medication that was needed, including putting bitter aloes on the nails of one boy in an attempt at stopping him from biting them, after breakfast. One day John Hitch who was Reg Hitch's sixteen-year-old brother was brought in by Mr White who was carrying him on his shoulder. John had somehow squashed his foot. I had the job of dressing and bandaging it and found a walking stick for him. This was then a daily chore for a week or more. Sometimes there were others who needed similar treatment for one reason or another.

I made most of the beds though, the older boys had to do their own on alternate days and I changed sheets once a week. Putting the top sheet to the bottom and a clean one on the top and a clean pillowcase each time. The boys had two blankets and a coloured cotton bedcover each, also an underblanket, which was flannelette. If they were cold they could ask for a third blanket but there were no eiderdowns and duvet as we know them now, were almost unheard of. The used sheets and pillowcases were put to the wash. We had a woman come one day each week to do all the school laundry, in the scullery where there was a boiler. We no longer sent baskets of laundry away to be returned already washed and ironed. I had a lot of the ironing to do with an electric iron usually in the dining room. Edith did some of it sometimes. I once overheard Miss Budding saying to Mother, "Edith is quick with the ironing but she is a bit slapdash, Brenda is slower, but more thorough". She didn't know I was within hearing. The only power plug was on the ground floor so we could plug the iron in. When I used it in Mother's room upstairs, it had to be plugged into the light socket, not a good idea really.

On Saturdays best suits had to be put out on the beds ready for boys to wear on Sundays. On Monday these had to have any spots cleaned off, were brushed, folded and put away usually in a chest of draws in the dormitory ready for next week, with if necessary a clean shirt and or collar. I sometimes used a cleaning fluid, but mostly a blue bag. This was a solid blue powder, which was square, about the size of a chalk used for the tip of a snooker cue. The blue block was wrapped in a piece of flannel dipped into cold water and rubbed on the spots on the black suits, before they were brushed. Any soiled shirts and collars were put to the wash. The collars had to be starched. Dormitory floors had to be mopped with a dry mop to take up the dust from the linoleum on the floor every day and the mop was then shaken out of the window. As boys had to hang dressing gowns on hooks or the door and put slippers on their bedside chair, it didn't take long to put the mop round the floors. Once each week a wet mop was used to wash the floors. A special galvanised bucket with soft soap and disinfectant in very hot water did the trick. The bucket had holes in half of the top, shaped in such a way that the water could be squeezed from the mop. It was not too difficult and scarcely took longer than the dry mop. There were five dormitories, so I took it in turn to use the wet mop. There were three landings with stairs in between that had to be polished weekly and mopped down daily with the dry mop. There were two baths and quite a number of basins that had to be cleaned every day and the two bathroom floors mopped with the wet mop.

I helped with darning boys' socks and sewing many buttons on to the shirts and pyjamas that had been put through the big mangle with wooden rollers that invariably took buttons off.

At the beginning and end of term I did all the packing and unpacking of the trunks that the boys all had to have, with their belongings in. One by one they came to the bathroom where some of the lockers were or on the landing where others were. The boy in question took his personal possessions away to put them where he could keep them. I put the clothes in the appropriate locker that had a name on, and made sure everything was correctly marked with the boy's surname and initials. Then made sure they were listed and I ticked each item off. Boys frequently arrived at the beginning of term with some things unmarked. I had to rectify this. At the end of term some things were sometimes missing with no accounting for whatever it was. During the term some boys had extra items of clothing sent to them so there was more to go into the trunk. This meant getting a boy to help me by sitting on the trunk to get it to close. Then labels had to be written on and fixed to the trunks.

When supervising the boys as they washed and dressed in the morning or prepared for bed at night, I usually stood at the door of the bathroom or dormitory knitting. Boys had to line up at the door when ready in their dressing gowns to go to the bathroom and again before returning to the dormitory. I did not supervise the older boys who had their washroom on the ground floor. Supervising them was mostly done by a master. Sometimes Winifred did this too. It was from her that I had the idea of knitting while supervising, because I saw her doing it. I had by then really got into knitting. I had made several jumpers for myself and later was asked by 'Uncle' of Waters Lane to make three pairs of socks for him. I had not previously knitted socks, so although I didn't use a pattern for jumpers, I had to for the socks. Uncle paid for the wool and paid me ten shillings for knitting the three pairs of socks.

Before Roy left we were very daring. I don't remember whose idea it was or who started it. I rather think it was Edith who started the ball rolling. It certainly was not my idea in the first place because I was always terrified we would be found out, but we never were. Edith visited Reg Hitch in his room, long after we were supposed to have, and in fact had, our light out. Reg had a soft spot for Edith. It had to be when Reg was on duty. At the same time, Betty's boyfriend David, and Roy came into our room. My father was no doubt out as he went to the Albion Hotel for a drink, which was where Betty's father was. He was either the owner or the manager. He and my father were friends. Mother would have been in bed as she always went to bed early. It didn't happen many times but our boys were well behaved. There was no jumping into bed on their part and they wore dressing gowns. It didn't stop plenty of hugs and kisses and although most enjoyable, not as much as it might have been because of the fear of being found out. I am sure the only reason we got away with it was because Reg was always on duty and was very willing to have Edith visit him!

Edith was still with us even after I had finished lessons but I can't remember for how long, and so was Betty, though she sometimes went home at the weekend like her younger brother.

When the new term started in September, Roy had gone and we were not able to keep in touch.

My father had a talk with me one day, explaining that he would never be any good to me as he wasn't academically very bright and never would be. A thing that sticks in my mind is that he said, "he will never be able to discuss a book with you". I thought that was a peculiar example to give at the time, but later I understood what he meant. I don't remember any allusion to the fact that he was coloured, though I have a feeling that at the back of his mind he didn't want a daughter of his to entertain the idea of what would then have been considered a very unsuitable mixed marriage. However, although not very happy with the situation, I accepted what he said and felt I must put up with not seeing Roy any more. I didn't have to be unhappy for long though because our new sports master, 'Sally' took a shine to me and it wasn't long before he became my boyfriend. He was only about a year or two older than I but looked every bit of twenty. He had been to the public school Harrow. Times were hard at home. His father had left and his Mother couldn't afford to keep him at school. He had therefore to leave and take a job. Everyone seemed to think well of him and no one seemed to mind when we became friends. He was of course, just the opposite of Roy, in many ways. One thing that struck me was that he was always very generous. For example, often buying cream meringues for me because he knew I liked them. I don't remember presents from Roy. I admit that I think he had very little pocket money. That had been another job I had done for my father when he was ill. I gave out the pocket money. Boys didn't have very much as my father tended to restrict them with regard to how much they had. The one thing I do remember Roy giving me was some crystallised guava fruits. He had been sent them from home. They were delicious and he shared them with me. I had never heard of them before and have not seen any since. They evidently grew on a tree in tropical America and can be used for making jelly. They must grow in the West Indies as Roy's home was on the island of Granada, which I had spent a lot of time studying, as I fondly imaged I would one day go to live there. Talk about childhood fantasies!

I did see Roy twice after he left. He returned just before or after Christmas to visit us, he still hadn't gone back to the West Indies. We went down to Emily's and while there I grabbed the wrong end of the poker that Roy had hold of. I didn't realise that it was still very hot after being in the fire, because it looked black. I burnt my hand badly and had to get some special yellow ointment from the chemist to put on it and then bound it up. For some while after I had to write with my left hand, it was too painful to try to use the right one. The only explanation I could give about it, was that I had grabbed the wrong end of the poker without thinking. No way could I say that Roy had hold of the other end, as we shouldn't have been there together. The second time he came was the last time. We managed to go outside at the back of the school to chat. I tried to explain to him that my father wouldn't allow me to keep in touch so the position was hopeless. I felt very mean and tried to be as gently as I could about it but I knew he was very upset. I didn't mention 'Sally', as I knew I was hurting him quite enough without adding insult to injury. Many, many years later I heard from Mother, when I once said to her that I wondered what had happened to Roy, that he was married and she thought had a family. She had kept in touch with his uncle, and said she thought Roy lived somewhere in Central America. Mother was always good at corresponding and keeping in touch with people. I was by then married and had a family. I was very pleased to hear that he was apparently happy.

In September 1934 we went to Cornwall. Uncle Lewis took us in his car. Travelling was much slower then, so we had to make a very early start. Winifred had woken me at five thirty in the morning and we eventually set off at seven. We were very loaded with luggage and a tent for four of us. That is, Uncle Lewis, Winifred, Sylvia and myself. We made our way towards Canterbury, eating a breakfast of sandwiches as we went. There was very little traffic at first and some of the roads were scarcely more than lanes. It was nothing like it is today. As we travelled through Kent there was a lot of beautiful scenery to be seen, including apple orchards. We stopped later in a lane to eat more sandwiches. I had been eating chocolate and apples in between because I found that sitting in the back of the car I felt car sick if I didn't' keep eating! We had been through Surrey and then through Salisbury and suddenly we were in Exeter and it was four o'clock in the afternoon. I had been to sleep. It seemed that the car engine needed some attention at that point so we stopped, but Uncle Lewis soon put it right and after buying some fruit we set off again. We travelled on over Dartmoor and thought we had never seen such beautiful countryside, in spite of the lovely countryside we had been through in Kent and Surrey. As we went on there was very little habitation at all, except for the occasional old cottage here and there. There were hills and valleys and streams. One place called Two Bridges had stepping-stones and water falls. It was all very picturesque. Then we saw many wild ponies and we stopped for another picnic to watch them and to look at the beauty which was all around. Finally we drove on to arrive in Perranporth at seven in the evening. We had been travelling for twelve hours and had covered about three hundred miles. We soon found our other sister Dorothea, who was working at the time as a waitress in a restaurant, which was only open for the summer season. She showed us where we could pitch our tent and we soon had it up and were wrapped in blankets and sleeping on ground sheets.

Uncle Lewis slept in the car and Dorothea went back to where she worked. The next evening when Winifred and Uncle Lewis had gone off for a walk, Sylvia, Dorothea and I were sitting chatting in the tent when we saw something was on fire and about three quarters of a mile away. Huge flames were leaping up in the sky and it was late enough to be otherwise dark. There were no street lights anywhere. Sylvia said we ought to go over to it to see if anyone was hurt as she was a nurse and might be able to help. This we did, only to find that it was a garage that had had three cars in it. Two had been rescued but the third one and the garage were completely destroyed. The fire engine came eventually but as it had come from Truro, which was nine miles away, we were there before it arrived. There had been a crowd there before us so as no one was hurt our help was not needed and we made our way back to the tent. We didn't stay there many days but we were able to see Dorothea each day while we were there. On the way home we spent a night in the tent at Sandy Bay. More of that later.

Plate Titles

Section Four

24) 1934. Peter in his tent.

25) 1934. Me holding Anthea, Jack and Eileen's baby.

26) 1934. Some of the boys at The College, in their Sunday suits. Michael can be seen on the extreme right, at the back.

27) As photo 26, but no Michael.

28) 1934. Georgie.

29) 1934. Boys in their sports clothes. Michael is standing second from the left.

30) 1934. Ernest (who played the piano) Reg, Edith and Mr White.

31) 1934. Me at Sandy Bay.

32) 1934. Winifred and Sylvia at Sandy Bay.

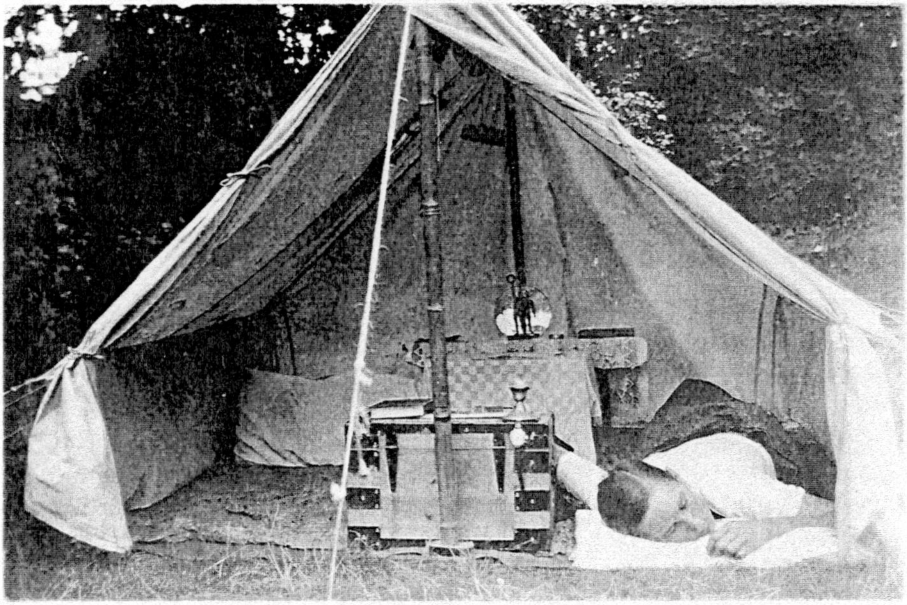

CHAPTER VI

WE WENT TO SANDY BAY AGAIN

During the winter months life went on much as usual. Edith and I often went to the stables. We somehow acquired breeches and hoped when we offered to help that we would be offered a ride but we were out of luck and our help was not often wanted either.

'Sally' and I spent quite a lot of time together one way and another and didn't have to be too secretive about it. He enjoyed being a sports master for a time including when we had snow and we all played in the snow.

However, he wanted something better and I became very tired of all the endless tasks that came my way. I wanted to get a job in a bank but I had no qualifications, so I thought the post office would be the next best thing. My father didn't think that was a good idea.

I arranged to go up to North London to my grandparent's home, where one Auntie was still living too. I put my hair up in a bun at the back of my head and had to use big long hairpins. I thought I looked really gown up. It was London, so a hat, that cost two shillings, and gloves that cost one shilling always had to be worn, and not sandals! I scanned the advertisements in the papers and went for a few interviews. I remember one I went to was up a narrow staircase where there was just one man who was a Jew. He said he would take me on. I am not even sure now what the job was, but my Aunty Amy wouldn't hear of it. One man on his own! It was not on.

I was still as naïve as they come! I found a job eventually in a large store in Hackney. It was called Parnells. There were four departments all staffed by women, no men, so I could live in. I was to work in the baby linen department. My Aunty Amy told me I wouldn't like it but I didn't listen. I was taken on for one month's trial. I had very little money but because I was to live in I had no living expenses. I had to buy and wear a long sleeved black dress. I shared a bedroom with another girl who was not much older than I. She had been there a while so could show me the ropes, so to speak. There were a few others who lived in. We had our meals together. The food was quite good. There was a dining room and a sitting room but nothing to do in the evenings or at the weekend. Most people went home or away at the weekends. We had Sunday off and a half day during the week. 'Sally's' Mother lived in Kensington and he was at home so came over to take me out, or I went over there. We went to the cinema and with his sister we went ice-skating. Sally even took me one day to the Albert Hall to watch the boxing, we sat up 'in the gods' as the very top stalls were called. It was an experience I couldn't forget. There were strict rules about being in by half past ten in the evenings. 'Sally' brought me back and we said our fond farewells on the doorstep at the back of the building where I had to go upstairs to the living quarters. If anyone who worked there saw us standing there talking, it was frowned on. Some Sundays I was invited to 'Sally's' home. I got to know his Mother and sister well. I remember staying in one Sunday. The girl I shared a bedroom with spent all her off duty time reading and knitting at the same time, which was more than I could do. She never seemed to go away or out.

The other person, who worked in the baby linen department, was in charge. She told me what to do. Clothes were in shelves that pulled out. I had to tidy the clothes. I also had to dust everything everywhere. We were never able to sit down while on duty. There was only one chair in the department and that was in front of the counter for customers. From nine to one and from two till six we were on our feet. Dinner was from one till two, while the store closed. When a window display was dismantled I had to help carry the 'dummies' that clothes had been on in the window, down to the cellar. That was where the ironing was done, so I had the job of turning anything that had been displayed, inside out and ironing it on the wrong side before turning it back, folding it and returning it to wherever it had come from. That included endless items of lingerie from other departments. All the price tickets were thrown into a box for me to sort, and although the first time I did it I had another girl to show me how, I mostly did it on my own. This I actually enjoyed, partly because I was able to sit on a stool in the cellar to arrange them all in numerical order in a huge wooden box. I had fondly imaged I was going to stand behind a counter and sell baby clothes to Mothers with small children, taking the money. I actually sold one thing the whole of the four weeks I was there. It was a busy Saturday afternoon. Every time a customer was shown a number of items, they were passed to me after to fold and put back where they belonged. Suddenly while the senior assistant was busy serving a customer another customer asked me how much a rattle was which was with some others on the counter. I told her it was six pence. It had a price ticket on it. She gave me the six pence and took the rattle. I passed the six pence on explaining what it was for. I didn't get to go near the cash till and the look I got, almost said, "you shouldn't have done it"! Some people never learn to say "thank you". By then I was really felling homesick and gave in my notice. I finished my month and was pleased to say, "goodbye".

There was one highlight that month. It was May 1935, the Jubilee year for King George V and Queen Mary. Everyone had a day off. Sylvia went to Ealing and it was arranged that I should join her. She was staying with Norwegian cousins of our cousins who live in Wales. It was a scorching hot day. Having stayed the night we set off quite early after breakfast. I don't remember where we went but we had a very good view amongst huge crowds of other people standing on a fairly wide pavement. We watched as the royal procession went by and I certainly saw the King and Queen. There were Union Jack flags everywhere and red, white and flue buntings all over the place. We spent the day watching all that went on including the lights that were lit especially for the occasion. Sylvia, who could always draw anything, drew a picture of St Paul's Cathedral, lit up with searchlights, on a matchbox. Later she made a lino cut of it, which I still have a picture of, made from it.

When I went home after that month, the job I had done at home was no longer available and I was told to find myself another job.

The governess job that Dorothea had previously had in Westgate was vacant. Because I was Dorothea's sister they took me on very readily. Because Dorothea had liked it so much, I was sure I would like it. However, not so. When Dorothea was there the children were, mostly school age. They were intelligent children from well to do families and had been living abroad. I think their parents were abroad. They went to school during term time. Dorothea would escort them there and fetch them after, and look after them in between.

When I went there, the children were toddlers, there were no older ones. In fact there were only two. The establishment was run by two spinsters who were sisters. I was not used to toddlers. I dressed them ready for breakfast and had little or no say about what went on at meal times as we all had meals together, the two spinsters, the two toddlers and myself. I took them out for walks, one in a pushchair, and put them in their beds for a sleep after dinner. Once they were in bed at night I was expected to darn their sock or do any other mending for them, in my so called bed sitting room entirely on my own. That didn't suit me at all. I think I only lasted about three weeks. Then home I went again! This time it suited my parents to take pity on me, as they needed someone to do the dining room chores. I was told I could stay if I agreed to do that.

All this time I kept in touch with 'Sally' and I think it is time I explained why he was called 'Sally'. He really had a rather ugly face, which included a nose that had been broken when boxing. He had a very charming smile though and a personality that appealed to most people. One day when he laughed out loud he opened his mouth so wide, I told him he looked like 'Aunt Sally'. He then explained that because his initials were SAL, that 'Sally' was his nickname. His first name was Steven and I sometimes called him Steve, but mostly he was Sally! We exchanged many letters. We even talked on the phone sometimes. I in a call box down the road, he at home. I knitted a scarf for him. The wool cost five shillings. He wanted it to be six feet long and fairly wide in double knitting, navy blue and white, which were his old school colours. He nearly always wore his 'old school' tie and was very proud of it.

During the time that I did the dining room chores, I had to wash all the cutlery. Not the plates though. I had to take them along to a lift which was near the top of the stairs that led to the lower ground floor where the kitchen was and put them in and send them down for Jesse to collect and wash them in the scullery. I used a sink, which was in the boiler room where the senior boys had their wash basins. There was always plenty of very hot water to which I had to add common household washing soda. There was no such thing as washing up liquid then. I had a wart on one finger. I had tried several of the usual remedies that were recommended at that time, one being a special black pencil that had to be made wet before application, all to no avail. I soon found, however, having my hands in the hot water to which I had added the soda, soon sent it on its way and it never returned! I do not remember what other duties there were but you can be sure there were some. My hair, which was getting very long, seemed less heavy when I plaited it and folded the plats round my head. I still had to use long hair pins to keep it up.

A couple of years before, when I seemed to be having too many headaches, Mother sent me to the local optician. My father was not very pleased as he had the bill to pay. I had been prescribed reading glasses and some slightly tinted ones for bright lights. I didn't use either a great deal and relegated them to a draw for many years fairly soon after, but I bought a pair of dark sunglasses for two shillings for use when I found the sun was too bright.

While it was still school holidays I went to Sandy Bay in Devon. It was not far from Exmouth near Budleigh Salterton. Uncle Lewis had by then a holiday bungalow there. Other bungalows were near by but not very near so we were fairly isolated. The location was not very well known at that time. It was where we had spent a night in a tent the year before. The beach could only be approached if we walked across the field from the bungalow and went down many steep wooden steps. The cliff face was red, something I had not seen before because in Kent they are all white. Uncle Lewis took five of us this time. Winifred, Reg, John Hitch, his brother and me. The journey was not as long as it had been the year before, but most enjoyable. While there, Uncle Lewis always had the wireless on while Sir Henry Wood conducted the proms. He was very keen on listening to them. Uncle Lewis had a good tenor voice. He was fond of music. While there we also had Bunch the dog with us. On the way home we met our second cousin Beryl we had been helping out at our school earlier on. She was driving her father's car. He was Uncle Cecil to us. He always had flashy rather super cars. With her was her moth Auntie Jesse. I am sure Beryl had deliberately engineered the meeting in order to see Reg. We stopped for a while to chat and take photos but as we were going in opposite directions we had to go on our way.

I am nearly sure Dorothea was at Perranporth again that summer and I have no idea what she did in between. She then came home.

During the next term I thought I would go to evening classes so that I could get a qualification that would give me a change to have a job worth having. I can't remember what I thought I'd like to study. I would have been better off if I hadn't bothered. I went two or three times and disliked it intensely.

By then letters from Sally had become very infrequent. When they did come he made excuses about too much overtime in the bank where he was working. I was getting to the point of despair. I loved Sally as much as I had previously loved Roy, and could not imagine that he had got to the point where I was no longer of any interest to him. Eventually in desperation, because I knew it would be no use asking, I decided to take myself off up to London to where he lived with his Mother and sister in Kensington. I had only a few shillings, certainly not enough for my faire to London, so I started walking. It was not long before a very kind lorry driver stopped to give me a lift. I didn't imagine I was taking a risk and had a very nice ride and a good chat. I told him where I intended to go and why. He took me as far as he was going towards where I wanted to go. I was very lucky. He gave me sixpence to help me pay my fare for the rest of the journey and tried not very successfully to extract a kiss from me as he let me out of the cab. I made my way to Mater as Sally always called his Mother, so I did too. She was very kind. She phoned my home to say I was there, let me stay a night and we had a good chat. It had taken me most of the day to get there partly because I had walked some of the way. When I got to London I had been into a Lyons teashop for a snack. I could not have easily got home again the same day. I had to accept the fact that Sally was not interested, but Mater told me I could visit her anytime I was near enough to do so. She ran a rather exclusive home for grownups of any age, who needed care and had the money to pay her fees. Some had their meals in their bedrooms, and some came to join the family meal table most of the time. There were usually about three or four in residence at a time, some quite long stay and others for a short time. Mater lent me money enough to get home. I had a very cool reception but very little was said.

Ray, who is and has been for many years by brother in law, came to the school as our last sports master. My sister Dorothea and he didn't waste much time deciding they were meant to spend the rest of their lives together. At least that was how I saw it, and how right they were.

My father's landlord died and his son inherited the school and land that surrounded it. The school fees had not been paid by many parents. This meant the rent for the premises could not be paid. The new landlord sent the bailiffs in. Everything was listed. Mother was able to claim a few things as her own under the 'wife's property act'. One such thing was a Chinese set of cups, saucers and plate's etc which had been a wedding present from some special friends who had lived in China. It is still in the family. Amongst things listed were watercolours that were family heirlooms. These were merely listed as pictures. Obviously those making the lists had no idea of the significance of those pictures. There were other pictures that were of no value or importance that were not even listed. Dorothea and Ray exchanged the heirlooms for the ordinary ones and they were wrapped in blankets, put into the back of Uncle Lewis' car and taken to a friend of Mother's who lived in Cliftonville near Margate. This was a friend who had lived in Tenterden when we lived not far from there.

Though we were only a few weeks into the new term, obviously the boys in the school had to go. Some went home. One boy who had been the worst of any of them to grumble about anything and everything, became the one to have the most to say about not wanting to leave because he liked being there!

Some boys, particularly those who had parents abroad, were sent to the school in Cliftonville where our previous vice principal then had his own school, and where Mary who had been our nursery nurse was the matron.

Plate Titles

Section Five

33) 1935. Winifred, Bunch and Lewis outside Lewis' bungalow at Sandy Bay.

34) 1935. Reg, Beryl (driver), John, Winifred and Lewis with Uncle Cecils' Car.

35) 1935. On the way back from Sandy Bay. Lewis, Auntie Jesse, Me, Reg, Winifred and John (seated).

36) 1935. Sally in the snow.

AGX 933

CHAPTER VII

THE BABIES HOSPITAL

I don't remember exactly where everyone went. I knew Michael was taken in by a friend, near by so that he could finish his term at St Lawrence College. Winifred was at one time with our grandparents and later with Lewis in the bungalow near Budleigh Salteron. It was sad to have to say "Good bye" to Emily, Walter and Jesse, but we kept in touch for a time. We got to the point where we had no food left, no money to get any with and of course no shops that would give us credit. Mother said about the food, "God will provide". She had such faith, and He did. Mother's friend where the pictures had gone, sent over a very adequate basket full of all kinds of food.

Uncle Edwin then sent money for the train fare for me to go to his home in Mumbles in South Wales. I think he must have done the same for my father and Dorothea, because I think they too were there for a very short time. I actually went on the seventh of February 1936. Uncle Edwin had lent me one pound and ten shillings. The fare cost one pound four shillings and eleven pence. I can't imagine how I was supposed to pay it back or if I ever did. I had my seventeenth birthday while there soon after. For my birthday I had thirteen shillings from various sources and a fountain pen from my brother Peter. Another second cousin, known as cousin Maggie sent me two shillings and six pence. She had done that each year since I was aged eleven and at school with another second cousin Joan in London, because she learned that my birthday was the day before Joan's and I was one year older. It was the last time I had the birthday money from her because I spoilt it by asking her to lend me money to take up a writing course. As an avid reader, I fondly imagined I could learn to write with a little helpful tuition. Cousin Maggie did reply to my request, saying she was sorry she couldn't help me, but I never heard from her again. Of course it is just possible that she didn't have my address as I had moved by the time I had my next birthday, but I don't think that was the real reason.

One thing I bought with my birthday money that year was quite a small round clock for only two shillings. It kept good time and was very useful to me for many years.

Uncle Edwin and Auntie Mary had extended their house from when I had stayed there when I was ten years old. They had Irene who was thirty-one, who was a qualified chemist and worked in the dispensary in Uncle Edwin's shop. Sybil who was twenty-seven who was not qualified but helped Auntie Mary as a housekeeper, and Edna who was a year older than I. She worked in the photographic department, in the darkroom, which was out in the yard at the back of the premises. They were all at home. John who, had earlier been at our school for a short while, was Edna's twin. He was I think, away from home by then but I am not sure.

The chemist shop was nearly twice the size it had been, as Uncle Edwin had taken over the next door premises which had previously been a bank. Upstairs there were more bedrooms, a large dining room as well as a breakfast room and a lounge. I think Uncle Edwin had an office too. By then Besta Papa, Auntie Mary's father had died and Besta Mama, her Mother had given up the house down the road to come to live with Auntie Mary. Besta Mama must have been getting on for eighty or more. She was a very sweet quiet white haired lady who still had her Norwegian accent. She spent a lot of time sitting near the window where she could see out to the road, crocheting white cotton bedspreads, with a fine hook. They had no garden, only a yard with one tree growing in the middle of it. There were other Norwegian relations near, whom we saw at times. Auntie Mary was a very hospitable person. Often her dining table had many people round it as well as her own family. She was very kind but a bit strict. I found it difficult to get up in the morning because supper was so late in the evening that I was late to bed. A few times I was so tired when it came to supper time that I had to excuse myself and go up to bed rather than stay for supper. Auntie Mary didn't like it if any one was late for breakfast. We had grace before each meal and family prayers taken by Uncle Edwin at the breakfast table before or after breakfast. Mostly he was in the shop or office except on Sundays. The Meeting House as the chapel next door was called was attended by many including all the family. Uncle Edwin took part in conducting it. He was a lay preacher and very keen on the Gideon Society.

There was one day when he went up to the British Industries Fayre in London. The King Edward VIII was being taken round. Uncle Edwin saw him pick up a pair of binoculars and when he had moved on, Uncle Edwin picked them up and said, "I'll have these please". He came home and told us he had a pair of binoculars that the king had looked through! It was as though he had won a gold medal, he was so pleased with himself!

I had arranged to go for an eighteen-month training at Fulham Babies Hospital. I was not able to go before May because one had to be at least seventeen and a quarter when starting.

I was only at Mumbles for two months, though looking back it always seems much longer. Uncle Edwin was in many ways like my father. He was two years younger and like my father wore a beard. Physically though they differed as Uncle Edwin was always slim and sprightly and lived well into his nineties. He was, however, frequently full of laughter and fun. In the evenings we sat round a table to play games. I remember Spelka, which as a game we had often played as a family in Mother's room when I was much younger. In some ways the modern equivalent is scrabble, but Spelka is a card game. There were various others but not playing cards as such. They were used by gamblers so were strictly taboo. Uncle Edwin didn't join in the games as he was too busy, often in his study, or he might sit reading while we played. Besta Mama would have gone to bed, so Auntie Mary, Irene, Sybil, Edna and Dorothea while she was there, and I usually played. If my father was there, it was not for long, so I am not sure where he was.

Ray came to visit Dorothea and quite soon she was at Monkton Wyld, near Charmouth in Devon. It is midway between Axminster and Lyme Regis. It was April before I went. I was sent for by Wendy and Geoffrey who wanted me to look after two children.

In the meantime I was at Mumbles enjoying myself most of the time. Of course I couldn't expect to be there for too long for nothing even if they were my Auntie and Uncle, so I was roped in to pull my weight by helping to do the spring-cleaning. This was Sybil's department. Sybil was not the brightest of people, that is why she was still at home helping Auntie Mary as housekeeper. When it came to spring-cleaning though she really knew how to go about it. Evidently it had been done regularly every year since she could remember. I, on the other hand, had almost never heard of it. At least never experienced it. In our school we seemed to move or change over rooms during the holidays from time to time and anywhere that needed decorating was done in its turn, in the holidays of course. Spring-cleaning was not part of my life, as such up to then. Sybil, usually called Sib and nicknamed Squib was an expert. Every single item had to be washed or dusted. Every nook and cranny had to be cleaned. Every bed stripped and cleaned, bedding washed and changed and replaced and so on. Poor Sib was fit for nothing at the end of the day, as she was not over robust. There was a carpet sweeper, brooms, brushes and dusters and polish, but I don't remember an electric cleaner. The whole procedure was to me, the 'fly in the ointment' as far as my stay was concerned. I hated every minute of that spring-cleaning. I was truly thankful that it didn't last longer than it did.

When I went to Monkton Wyld, it was to Monkton Wyld Court. It is only a small hamlet. Wendy and Geoffrey had taken the house as a country guesthouse, cum smallholding. Wendy I had known since I was nine. She was a friend of my second cousin Beryl and had been at our school during one summer holiday to teach English to foreign students. She was at that time nineteen and had since trained as a musician and was well qualified. Geoffrey, whom she had married, worked in the Bank of England. He was amongst many who were made redundant during the thirties and used his redundancy money with that of the sale of their house in Surrey where they lived, to buy Monkton Wyld Court. I had met Geoffrey once before, while on a journey with Winifred and Uncle Lewis in 1934 just before Francis their eldest child was born in June. We had called in on our way to or from somewhere. By the time I arrived at Monkton Wyld Court, Francis was twenty-two months. Anthea was the daughter of Jack and Eileen who had been at Broadstairs at our school, at least Jack had been and Eileen often visited. She was twenty-one months. Jack and Eileen had gone to West Africa and left Anthea with Wendy and Geoffrey. I was therefore asked to look after these two small children. There is nothing like being thrown in at the deep end.

My experience of children of that age was nil. I had no idea even how to change a nappy, let along anything else, and they both had to wear nappies. They had been looked after for a while by a young German girl who was leaving so I had been asked to fill in while someone else was found. At that time there was a cook, a chauffeur and a dining-room maid, all of the 'downstairs' variety, who slept over the stables. I had to wash, dress and carry both children plus a very large soft toy doll belonging to Anthea down to the children's dining room for breakfast early in the morning, making quite sure they made no noise, because I was told, the guests must not be disturbed. The cook sent in what she thought was suitable for the children and except to make sure that they had some milk to drink, I had no idea what they should have. They played in the nursery or garden if it was fine, with much potting and changing of nappies, mostly a waste of time, then after drinks of orange juice at mid-morning I put them into their prams and left them for their morning sleep in the cottage garden which was well away from the house so that they would not be disturbed. The cottage was the annex that belonged to the house. It was rented by Miss Harvey, a lady of means who had Lesley living with her as her companion. Lesley was a spinster aged about forty-eight. The daughter of a doctor, who was no longer alive. I never heard her mention her Mother though I knew her well for the next forty or so years. When the children awoke from their midday sleep it was Lesley who heard them crying first, and she who saw to them. In fact she was wonderful, she instructed and helped me beyond any imagination, and she was a guest. Lesley and Miss Harvey came down to the house each evening for dinner but apart from that they lived in the cottage.

I saw very little of the guests as I spent most of my time with the children. The nursery was on the top floor. It had skylight windows, which were large, and two small high up slit windows that looked out on to the front garden. It was very large so I slept in there as well as the two children and they played in the garden quite a lot of the time. There were fourteen bedrooms. On the top floor was a bathroom with just a bath in it, where I bathed the children, also six double bedrooms with a large walk–in linen cupboard. This was Dorothea's domain as she was the housekeeper. There were not many guests just at that time as it was the Easter period. I could read quite a lot, as there were plenty of books I was able to borrow and although I spent time outside with the children while they were playing I was not expected to play with them. There was Biddy the dog, a very intelligent mongrel. It was very clear that she understood quite a number of words and other signs, without being specially taught them. There was a very beautiful longhaired tabby cat called Tim. Sometimes Geoffrey would have Tim on his shoulders even at meal times and as he went to put his fork into his mouth, Tim would put out a paw in an attempt to hook the food from the fork. Tim was particularly fond of runner beans and when eating them Geoffrey often allowed him to share his beans in this way. He was a much loved pampered cat and often slept on Wendy and Geoffrey's bed or if it was a bit cold, found a cosy nook in the hot cupboard. Dorothea had a bedroom on the top floor next to the hot cupboard and as a lover of animals had no objection if Tim found her bed to sleep on. There was also an English Setter but I don't think they had it very long. There were horses in the paddock. Both Wendy and Geoffrey rode well. Furzey was the gardener who also milked the two cows that were kept for their milk. They also had pigs and goats.

There was an artesian well, which supplied all the water that was needed, on a slope where there were trees and shrubs behind the house. There was never any trouble with the water. There was also a sewage system where it all went eventually to the stream that ran along the bottom of the paddock which slopped gently down to it, but in the centre of the paddock was a purifying plant that was purpose built. The man who did it showed how confident he was by taking a cup to the steam and drinking it. I am sure it was alright to do so, but I don't think I could have done.

In the stable building there was a battery house. The batteries were kept charged and from them the electricity for everywhere came. In the house, the stable block, the garage and I think the cottage. There was no shortage of light or power

On the first floor there was a bathroom and toilet and eight bedrooms. These varied a little in size but were all double rooms, and one was extra large with a small room leading from it. All the bedrooms had their own plumbed in basin with running hot and cold water.

On the ground floor, entering the front door, in the hall one could see a spinet standing opposite, and a room to the right was at that time the bar, where guests could get their drinks. Along a wide passageway there was a cloakroom, with wash basin, hooks for coats, and inside a toilet. To the right was the large drawing room and to the left very large round hot water radiator pipes, above which was a window looking out to the back of the house and the drive that continued from near the front door to beyond the house where the stable block and garage were. By the garage was a petrol pump with petrol for one shilling and two pence per gallon. Back in the house, past the drawing room was the dining room. Round the corner from there was a door that led out into the garden where the terrace was. At the end of the passage way to the left was a large alcove where Geoffrey had his desk with a window over it so it was known as the office. Finally there was a door through which were the kitchen quarters and the children's dining room. To the right was also a door at the bottom of the back stairs. They were not very wide and were made of wood. The front stairs were between the front hall and the cloakroom. They were very wide and made of stone. They went to the first floor only, where as the back stairs continued after the first floor to the top floor. There was a hatch from the children's dining room to the pantry, where dining room washing up was done and crockery and other things were kept. Along the passage of stone tiles was the kitchen through which one went to the scullery. The passage also led on to a back door and there was another back door out of the scullery. In the kitchen was a high fixed dresser with draws and cupboards under. Two large deal tables, one by the window and one in the middle of the room. Floor to ceiling cupboards were either side and well back, from two Aga cookers on which all the cooking was done.

The gravel terrace had grass either side of it and some flower beds. Steps led down to a grass level and more steps to more grass that sloped away to a large patch of rough grass. With the house behind you a tennis court could be seen over to the right. Going out of the front gate, turning left the lane went past the church and the cemetery and a cottage occupied by the church caretaker, also a memorial. Further down the lane was the orchard that belonged to the guesthouse. There were trees in there and that is where the billygoat had his hut. There were other goats too but more of that later.

While I was there for that month, I wore what I liked. Most of my clothes were passed on or given to me. When I put the black dress on that I had had to wear in the shop the year before, Wendy thought, it or may be I in it, looked terrible, so I didn't wear that any more! I did have a very nice two piece I had been given, not new, but new enough for me. It was a mid navy, machine knitted and made of good quality wool. It was inclined to cling, at least the skirt that had a fairly wide elastic waistband was, but my figure was such at that time that I could take it! Because I was there only one month that year I will leave the further story of Monkton Wyld Court for when I came again.

It was another year before I returned to Monkton Wyld Court. I went from there in May 1936 on the train from Axminster to do the training at Fulham Babies Hospital that I had arranged to do about four months before. On arrival I was shown to my room which was shared with one other probationer nurse as we were called. Nurse Cheshire told me a little about what went on and what to expect and helped me to get my uniform. She also showed me how to fix my headwear. It started off as a plain piece of white starched cotton and had to be carefully pleated at the back of the head and pinned so that it would hang down at the back and no hair would show. I was warned never to leave it 'til the morning to make up a cap, it would take too long and there was never enough time. We had a supper meal and I was told to get up when called at ten past six in the morning and to be on the ward by six thirty. The night nurse did the calling, rushing from one room to another and hastily saying. "ten past six Nurse Varley, ten past six Nurse ….." Whoever it was who was sharing my room, and no one was ever given a second call. Nurse Cheshire became quite a friend to me but we didn't use first names. There was a very stern strict Matron. A very kind sweet, but firm Sister, two Staff Nurses, one on day duty and one on night duty. There were only a few other nurses. I am not sure how many as there were only two wards. One had twelve cots in it and was for babies up to the age of one year. The other had six cots for older babies up to two years. The training was meant to be for eighteen months, after which one could offer a certificate to say one was qualified to be a nursery Nurse or Nanny. There were many strict rules and regulations. We worked ten-hour days. One might have two hours off either during the morning or the afternoon or from six O'clock in the evening. We had half an hour for breakfast and an hour for dinner, twenty minutes for tea, and later after coming off duty at eight o'clock, supper. Matron usually presided over the meals, saying grace before we started, and one had to be very careful about how one behaved and because we stood in awe of her there was very little conversation at the table.

On Sunday we had four hours off because we were expected to go to church. Matron even asked sometimes if we had been. On Sunday I could walk along to Kensington High Street and up through Church Street. There was a church half way up and Sally's Mater lived a bit further up in a turning off Church Street. Mater always made me welcome and I often walked to save the pennies, though I sometimes used the underground especially when returning at night. As I pass the church I reckoned I had 'been to it'. I wasn't asked if I had been in it, and I though it was nothing to do with her. She even asked which church I had been to. I was glad she didn't ask me what the sermon was about!

We had regular lectures, as often as not in our free time, because if we happened to be off duty when the lecture was due we had to attend just the same. I must say, although I thought some of what we were told was somewhat nonsensical, I didn't dislike the lectures because Sister took them, and we were sitting down, whereas while we were on duty we never sat down. The first duty in the morning was to change and feed your allotted patient. The feeds were put up in the bottles by Sister or a staff nurse and metal tags with very plain numbers on white discs were put on the necks of the bottles. The number would refer to the number on the cot of the baby who had to have it. We didn't pick the babies up to feed them. We turned them on their sides propped the pillow under their heads and tucked a bib under their chins. We must hold the bottle throughout a feed, never let the baby take hold of it, though some did put their hands round the bottle. We sat them up still in the cot holding their backs and fronts very carefully for them to get rid of their wind. Some of those in the ward for bigger babies were able to take groats, a fine porridge. Some that were cutting teeth, if well enough were propped up and given a rusk.

During the first hour the night nurses were still in the ward, as all the babies had to be washed as well as fed, so it was all hands to the pump, so to speak. I was soon shown how to make the cots and change any sheets that needed to be changed, as well as how to feed and change the babies. Being the junior, at first I had to dust every cot rail and locker in the ward and then go into the sluice room to rinse off all the nappies, that we had to call sundries, ready for them to go to the laundry. On the first day, again because I was the junior, I had to stay on the ward when everyone went to dinner. I had never in my life held or handled such small babies and was very afraid I would hurt them. One baby that cried, I had been told to pick up if he did. Sister heard it and came to my rescue explaining that babies were, as a rule tough and liked to be held firmly. In some cases if they cried a lot they could have a little boiled water, but all feeds were given at regular times and the times strictly adhered to. No dummies were every used.

There were plenty of other jobs to do as no one was allowed to be idle for one single minute. We had stiff white collars that had to be fixed on with a front and back stud. Dresses were blue and white striped, on top of which we had large white aprons that came up at the front with wide shoulder straps and they had to be tied together with tapes at the back. There was a special way to do this. Aprons had to be changed every day. We also had stiff white cuffs. The dress sleeves were long so the cuffs fitted over at the wrists. When any kind of washing of hands or anything else was done, the cuffs slid off and the dress sleeves had to be rolled up. There were several basins with running hot and cold water in the ward and there was much washing of hands, as they had to be washed after almost every task.

One had to have a pen in one's top pocket at all times. These would be fountain pens, as no biros or such like existed then. The pens were for charting temperatures. I soon learned how to take babies temperature as this was done at least twice each day.

Only a few of the babies seemed to be really ill, but they must have had something wrong to be there. One or two were there simply for loss of weight so much daily weighing went on. None were allowed to stay more than three months. I think two died while I was there but I don't know why and only remember one of them. He was three or four months old. One ten month old was one of a twin and was kept as long as possible because her Mother found it too difficult to cope with two at once. She was a really lovely baby. Little John as we all called him was very small and very wiry. In fact he was quite a job to hold on to when he chose to scream and kick as he often did, but we all loved him. The cots were pushed out into the garden when the weather was suitable. This was easy as they all had wheels on the legs of the cots. Little John could cry with fury and work his way up the cot and get his head through the bars. So special sausage like bolsters had to be made and put round the inside of the bars to stop him. One baby had Spina bifida. I was horrified when I was shown the gaping wound at the base of the spine.

One baby was very small and only about two months old. Her Mother was only thirteen years old, and the poor baby was very deformed from the waist down, had a cleft palate, which meant she was difficult to feed and had to have special large teats on her feeding bottles. They thought she was deaf too. I discovered that she was blind. I noticed that any baby, who was awake when I dusted the rails of the cot, would watch my hand as it went along. This baby never did. I told Sister what I thought so she came along to test the baby and agreed that I was right. After she had been with us for three months, she had to be sent to the general hospital. We were told she hadn't lived there long because they didn't know how to cope with her.

After I had been working in the larger ward for some weeks. I was sent to work in the ward where there were slightly older babies. These all had to have webbing restrainers on as they might stand up, or try to climb out of their cots. They were tied to either side underneath the cots with tapes, and were a harness that was tied up at the back of the child. They were spoon fed babies but didn't feed themselves, and drank from cups. At breakfast time it was groats, to be spoon fed, then half a slice of fried bread cut into small squares. Every child was supposed to finish every piece. I was forever being told off because I was too slow, always the last with whoever I was feeding. What was not know by Sister, or the staff nurse in charge, was that the other nurses usually threw away the last of the fried bread, if time was going on, rather than be told off for being too slow. You can't make a child eat more quickly than it wants to. On one occasion a child came in with diphtheria. Because I had had it as a child I was told it must be my patient while it was there until arrangements could be made for her to be sent to the isolation hospital. She was obviously very ill and I was pleased to be able to see to her. I also had to have a swab taken of my throat in case I was a carrier. Fortunately it proved negative and she was only with us a very few days. While attending to her a special gown and mask had to be worn. I felt quite important! Mothers of children came to visit them. A screen had to be put up for them to look through at their child. They were not allowed to go near or touch the child, or let the child hear them speak or see them. What a shame! But that was the rule, so not many came, and if they did, it was rarely more than once. The exception was very tiny premature babies who were being breast-fed. Mothers came in to feed, gradually coming less frequently until their supply had ceased to exist and the babies were then fed with a bottle. The staff nurse or a senior nurse usually saw to them. When babies went home the Mothers were advised to put something white on their own heads because their baby might not know them, and in that way had the sort of thing they were familiar with, to look at, and were less likely to cry.

When I had time off I was often too tired to do anything. I went to bed early and spent time reading. We could send our laundry, particularly our uniform, away so there was no washing to do. A day off meant I could go out so I took myself off to Mater as often as not. There were a few occasions when Sally and his sister Mary and others would join forces to go to the pictures or ice-skating. I had grandparents to visit too but the journey to North London where they were was rather far and therefore expensive on the underground or bus and I couldn't walk as far as that, so I didn't go many times.

After I had been at the hospital a few months and was getting used to the strict routine, a new probationer arrived. As the last one to come I was told to take her under my wing and show her what to do and what to expect. Sister had her table in the middle of the ward where at times she sat working. We seldom saw Matron, except when she did rounds with a doctor, or if called to her office, except at meal times. Sister missed nothing and although there were a few times when she put me wise as to how I should go about helping a new person, it wasn't long before she told me I was doing well and added, "you like teaching, don't you?" and when I agreed she added, 'I can see you do".

There was a very special procedure when a baby was admitted. Everything had to be prepared before it was taken from it's Mother, right down to a mackintosh cape and carbolic lotion. Then, take the temperature, report to Sister and eventually return the clothes to the Mother. They all wore hospital clothes while in hospital. The one I had to admit had such a thick crust of scurf that |I couldn't get it all off at the first go. I imagine it's head had never been properly washed from the day it was born, or at least very soon after.

After about four months or more I was put on night duty. By then I had in a way got used to the idea that Sally didn't want to see me, and although I had accepted the fact, I once found he had another girl with him and that really upset me. I think up to then I had lived in hopes that he would come round to me again. The night duty didn't help because it was a very lonely job. There was one staff nurse that I couldn't take to who was in complete charge once Sister had gone off duty at about eleven o'clock at night. Up 'til that time Sister helped feed some of the babies as there were too many for just two of us to cope with. Everyone had to be fed and changed. I had to put out two plates of dinner into the oven in the kitchen to warm. The staff nurse was due to go and have hers at twelve midnight. I was due to have mine at half past twelve. Invariably she was late going, which meant I too went late, so by the time I got to mine, it was just like a plate of charcoal. It was useless to say anything as nothing was done about it. While the staff nurse was off the ward it was usually quiet but there might be one baby for me to keep quiet with a bottle of water, otherwise I was found another job. Between after my half-hour for dinner and four o'clock I had all kinds of jobs. Most of it was in the sluice room where there were various bits of brass to clean. There were little woolly garments that had to be carefully washed by hand. There were tapes or buttons to sew on to other garments and other fiddley little jobs. There must never be an idle moment. At four o'clock it was a twenty minute tea break during which I spent half my time dropping asleep and coming to a couple of minutes later with a start for fear of taking too much time.

We started changing and feeding babies very early in the morning and then the day nurses came on duty to help and take over. We went off duty at eight o'clock and had our breakfast. We had to be in bed no later than eleven in the morning except when we had two nights off once each fortnight. Then we could go away or return for the night no later than half past ten. In the lectures that were given we had a lot of information that was common sense. But not many people have much common sense so it all had to be written down in black and white, so to speak, and learned. Some of it was as if one was back in school. Headings were, Punctuality, Obedience, Truthfulness, Loyalty, Cleanliness, Tidiness, Quickness one must be very quick when doing anything but one must never run, Quietness, Gentleness Observation. Method and Forethought. Under General Ward Work one is told exactly where every thing should be put and how and in what order everything should be done. Carbolic was the disinfectant used then, diluted to a given strength according to what one was doing. Under General Care of Babies we were given a timetable for babies at home because we were being trained to be nursery nurses. Then there were headings such as Clothing, Bathing, Sleep, Exercise, Regular Habits, Quietness, Warmth, Feeding and Feeding Bottles. Finally it was how to cope with a sick child. What to look for and what to do about anything that was wrong and always to be patient.

I didn't finish my stint on night duty. I became thoroughly disillusioned. I had a cough, which wasn't very helpful on nights and in desperation I made it out to be worse than it was. Eventually I was released from my contract on medical grounds.

With no home to go to I sought refuge with 'Auntie' at Waters Land. She was as usual kindness itself. In no time the country air and her care put me right, even if it was November. I was there for two weeks. While I was there 'Grandad' died. 'Grandad' who was 'Uncle's' father had been living with 'Auntie' and 'Uncle' for some years. When 'Auntie' had laid him out, she took me upstairs to the bedroom for me to get my first glimpse of a grown up dead. Only his head was visible. It was an experience! It was then considered that 1 was most useful to 'Auntie' as 1 helped her with the preparations for the wake and was able to stay in their cottage while they and their family went to the funeral. I made sure the fire was all right and the kettles on the boil on their return.

I scanned all newspapers for a job while there and replied to a few. I was offered an interview for one that was to train as a housekeeper in Bayswater. I went to the interview and was offered the job which, I was able to take at once. I may have visited Water's Land when passing through that way, while 'Auntie and Uncle' were still there, but I don't think 1 stayed there again. Until many years later when they had both gone, and Mary was there.

CHAPTER VIII

Housekeeping

Going up to London again was just what 1 wanted, at least I thought I did. 1 still hankered after Sally though 1 knew it was useless. At least 1 could still visit Mater who lived only walking distance from where my new job was. 1 had no uniform so 1 wore what I liked. I was living in so had no expenses in that way and was paid ten shillings each week. This was an improvement on the seven shilling and six pence I had had while nursing. Although in some ways it was almost slave labour rather than training, it was not so hard as nursing had been and there was no night duty.

The establishment was three tall London houses made into one. It catered for business ladies. Everyone had their own bedroom even if it was half of what had been a large room partitioned off to make it into two. I had one such room and saw almost nothing of the person who was in the other half. There was room for sixty-four. It was owned by two maiden ladies, both about in their fifties It was said that both had lost what might have been their husbands in the first world war. Although they interviewed me, they were rarely there and I saw almost nothing of them. There was a manager housekeeper in charge. She was often in the office and gave all the orders. She was a pleasant person and very well suited to the job, I for get her name. There was an assistant housekeeper who was very nice and a second assistant not much older than 1. We all got on well together. Duties started early. There were plenty of other workers, mainly cleaners and kitchen staff. I had the job of seeing that the writing tables in the lounges had clean blotting paper and that the inkwells were full, that curtains had been correctly pulled and none needed repairing. That cushions and chair covers were all in order. I must report anything amiss.

By seven four of us were in the serving room, serving breakfasts. Cooked breakfasts came up in the lift from the kitchen. The residents came to the hatch for whatever they wanted and there was a certain amount of choice. Quite a number had porridge though there was Force to be had. They were all gone to work by eight o'clock and we four sat down to a table that was in the middle of the dinning room that had been cleared and reset for us. At nine o'clock I had to be in the office most mornings as there were bills to make out that I copied from a book. Only the four of us had a midday meal and because we had to work most evenings, serving the evening meals, we often had time off in the afternoon. I had a day off each week and Sunday afternoons after serving midday meal, as there was no evening meal on a Sunday. Other duties consisted of getting the sheets from beds Mondays, sorting and listing the laundry ready for it to be collected in hampers. At the end of the week, the clean laundry that was returned had to be looked through carefully as well as counted in case there was mending to be done. They had a sewing machine with an attachment for darning that 1 was taught to use. I did much darning and patching of linen, that included tablecloths and serviettes.

In my room which had a bed and a small table, a wardrobe and a chest of draws. I had a gas fire that had to have a shilling put in a slot for it to work. As I was there during the winter I needed to have the fire on at times, particularly when I needed to dry my very long thick hair. The assistant housekeeper I forget her name too had her room next to mine. It was a genuine, single room not one that had been partitioned off. I often went in there for a chat with her. She was really kind to me. I think I sometimes had to help with the flower arranging and there must have been a few other duties but I cannot call them to mind. When a light bulb needed renewing they were a bit surprised when I offered to do it saying I had done it before. That saved a man having to be called in. They were more surprised still when 1 offered to mend a fuse asking if I was sure I could do it, which I could. But the thing that had them laughing was when 1 said I could change the washer on a tap if they would show me where to turn the water off and give me the necessary tools. I insisted I could do it and they calmed down once I had done it but still thought it funny that 1 could. I have a feeling that I had never actually changed a washer before but 1 had watched it being done enough times to be quite confident that 1 could, which of course I did quite successfully!

While I was there I hired a typewriter and had a book with instructions and exercises in it. I wanted to be able to type efficiently. I managed about thirty words a minute if they were small words and I had practised the same ones often enough but I didn't seem to be making fast enough progress for my liking, so I returned the machine after a few months. It cost more than I was prepared to part with.

The so called training course was for six months, so I was there until May 1937 when Wendy asked me to return to look after the children at Monkton Wyld Court.

In the mean time I did many things while still in London. I frequently walked along the Bayswater Road to Marble Arch, which was not very far. I loved to go into Selfridges and just look round. I could go upstairs, I think on an escalator where there was a free information desk. You could ask about anything past or present or from anywhere It was most useful. There were a lot of pianos in one department which I admired as there were all makes and sizes. On the ground floor there were waterproof watches exhibited in a water tank of fish. They were something quite new at the time and cost five pounds each. Quite a sum of money at that time. I stood fascinated just looking at them! Sometimes I went into a large store. 1 think it was called Whiteley which was just behind Selfridges. They sold every kind of piece of linen imaginable from sheets, pillows and their cases to table and tray cloths, serviettes and other pieces like dressing table sets.

Sometimes I walked through Hyde Park. I seldom used a bus or underground unless I was going a long way to visit relations. In the Park there was much to be seen. Ponies and traps horses and posh carriages. Nannies in uniform with their young charges usually in big high prams and perhaps a not quite so small child dressed up in coat, hat and gloves, walking sedately by their side. People riding on horses could also be seen in what was known as Rotten Row, a track especially for the horses that was not too hard for their feet. I also walked along to Notting Hill to go down Church Street to Kensington High Street where could go into the sales in Harrods and Daniel Neils. I bought a hat in Harrods and wore it a lot. In London a hat and gloves must always be worn and I even had a bit of a heel on a pair of navy court shoes that went well with my navy wool suit. Another two piece suit I wore a lot was a brown velvet skirt and short jacket passed on by Sally's sister Mary who was about my size. It was not any hardship to walk, particularly if I could save two pence. There were taxis in which a ride could be taken, for six pence, but not for me. I could never spare that much to take me a short distance. I did use the underground to go to see relatives. During that year I visited Grandma Williams as we called her to distinguish her from our other Grandma who lived in Stamford Hill with Grandpa and Auntie Amy. 1 had to take the last part of the journey by bus. She was ill with consumption and had been for nearly two years. She was as was usual then, bed ridden. I read to her while 1 was there and she died not all that long after. I can't remember just when but I was not expected to go to the funeral.

Another visit was to Carshalton where my second cousin Beryl was with her parents at the time. Uncle Cecil was my Father's cousin and his wife was Auntie Jesse. They had a lovely large bungalow and 1 stayed the night. Beryl did me proud in the morning by bringing breakfast to me in bed on a tray. I felt really honoured to be treated do well. Beryl had a brother Dennis who rode a motor bike. I had never been on one so he gave me a pillion ride. I thought it was great and he complimented me by saying I rode well because I went with the bike when he went round corners. He was very experienced so 1 had no fears. He had started to ride a motorbike when he was only fourteen, one could at that time but he was so small for his age that he had to carry his birth certificate with him. He was always being stopped. By the time I had my ride he must have been nearer thirty, than twenty.

Uncle George Auntie Edith and my cousin Phillip lived in Highgate near Muswell Hill in North London. The first time I went there I only saw Auntie Edith. It was one day in the week. I arrived very late in the afternoon because 1 had great difficulty finding the way. Auntie Edith was very kind and produced a splendid meal on a tray for me. I was then invited to go on a Sunday when Uncle George and Phillip would be there. Uncle George was Mother's elder brother. He was a big tall man. He had a very good job as accountant to the Treasury in some way. In spite of being well off. I never thought of him as being generous, We never had seen much of any of them, though Peter my brother stayed there at least once. Phillip was a little older than 1 but not much. He was an only child. When I visited for Sunday dinner Auntie Edith was a good hostess. She had a very lavish meal on the table. Everything being as one would imagine, of the highest order. Phillip was then a medical student though he never did become a doctor. I well remember him enlightening us on the subject of a case he was involved in. The case was a bisexual. The sort of thing that was virtually unheard of outside medical circles at that time. I don't remember ever seeing them again. They later moved up North somewhere, and although I know Phillip was married, he had no family and certainly did not live to the age of retirement.

Another visit was made to Eltham where Uncle Telford lived. He was in fact another cousin of my Father so was I suppose a second cousin to me but we always spoke of him as Uncle Telford. He was an artist and seemed to me to be a typical Varley. I can remember nothing of his wife but I. know he had two sons John and Jimmy because they were always on our family Christmas list, when we were younger. The boys were much older than I, in fact may have been older than my eldest sister. I remember only one thing about that visit. I don't even remember whether or not I met John and Jimmy. Uncle Telford showed me the family tree, I had not seen it before. He said he had my name and birth date on it but not Michael's, and asked me what it was so that he could fill it in.

Earlier that year King George V had died in January and during the year the newspapers were full of King Edward VIII and Mrs Simpson. In December came the abdication and while 1 was still in Bayswater on 12th May 1937 1 was able to see the procession after the coronation of King George VI. It was of course spectacular and very memorable.

I did a lot of other things during the year that I spent in London some while still at the hospital and some while at Bayswater. Anytime I had nothing to do and didn't want to walk in the shops or the parks I went to see Mater and at times helped her with the guests she had staying. One person I often sat with in her room and chatted to her. She was probably in her thirties and suffered with depression. She liked me to come for a chat and told me I had missed my vocation, as I ought to have gone in for nursing because she thought 1 was kind! I could never have entertained being a nurse like my sister Sylvia after hearing some of her experiences. It was the last thing that appealed to me. As usual I forget her name but she gave me a beautiful red silk scarf, which I still have and treasures.

When walking it was not unusual to see pavement artists who hoped to be given a few coins for their art. Sometimes they were war casualties with may be, one arm or one leg. Many wounded were not at that time fitted with false limbs so anyone with one leg used crutches and had the empty trouser leg pinned up. It was not an unusual sight, There were many plane trees in London as well as others but 1 hadn't remembered seeing the plane trees in the country and because they were always tall they seemed to be conspicuous. If walking in Kensington Gardens there was the round pond where children could sail their toy boats and the Serpentine went into Hyde Park where during the summer many people went swimming. Another thing one saw was an organ grinder. He pushed his barrel organ and stopped in the middle of any of the side streets off the main road where there were houses. He had a monkey on his shoulder and he wound a handle to make the organ play music. Coins were thrown out of windows into the street, which he collected. Children sometimes came out to watch and would pick up some of the coins for him. When these ceased to be forthcoming in one street he went on to another one.

Harold was a boy who was much the same age as I was. We never called him Harold, always by his surname. He was not a boy friend as such, but a friend and a 'bit of a lad"' He was at our school and had only a Mother. He had to leave when he was fourteen because his Mother couldn't afford to keep him at school any longer. He certainly had a good brain but sometimes it led him the wrong way. We knew he had a good job after he left but he came back to visit us so many times that we wondered how he could afford the train fare. It eventually transpired that in fact he couldn't and had been getting away with buying a platform ticket each time he travelled. It caught up with him and he was, as we called it 'locked up". But not for long. He soon surfaced and while I was in London I saw him a number of times, not alone. He always had others with him. He was forever the life and soul of the party. He had been just the some on his visits as an 'old boy" returning to the school. In fact he started and tried to run an 'old boys' association for the school and although a few ties were manufactured, I don't know who had them or what else happened and it never really got off the ground. 1 well remember on one of his visits some of us were at supper but no grown ups were present. Suddenly food was being thrown about. Of course Harold started it and he was impossible to stop. I could do nothing. They did clear up after but I can't think what it was all in aid of and no one had been drinking. We only ever had water in our dinning room. In London he introduced me to a Chinese Restaurant and to how to use chopsticks. I hadn't fancied the idea at all but he could be very persuasive and I enjoyed it in the end. There were other restaurants that we vent to. I don't remember who else came. Most likely Edith sometimes as she knew Harold and was in London at that time. There was Lyons Corner House and the A.B.C. both popular inexpensive places to go to eat. Sometimes I went in one of them by myself.

Woolworth's was a favourite place to look round with everything no more than six pence but they didn't have any restaurants in them then. The Crystal Palace was burnt down during that year. 1 had seen it at a distance but had not been into it. The smoke could be seen for miles around and I remember seeing it but not where from. When it came to Christmas in 1936, the last one seemed a lifetime away. I had no home to go to and although I probably knew at the time, I now have no definite idea of where the other members of the family were. I do remember three of us sitting down to a Christmas dinner in Bayswater where I was working. The fourth member of the upstairs staff had gone home and the residents didn't have a midday meal arranged for them and as it was a Friday a lot of them were away for the weekend. Edith was at that time in lodgings in another part of London and invited me to join in with their evening party. There was a long table and a good spread of food which I was pleased to be able to partake of even if Edith was the only person I knew.. It was very kind of her landlady to include me but I felt like a fish out of water.

In February I had my birthday. It was on a Sunday. Of course there was no post. I had had a letter from Mother the day before, but no one where I was knew, and I didn't tell them till the next day, when I had more post. It was my half-day that Sunday so after dinner I walked round to Mater's to spend the rest of the day there. She didn't know till I told her either. Sally wasn't at home, only his sister Mary. Not the sort of birthday I like to remember but somehow it sticks in my mind. Mary was slightly younger than I was but one wouldn't ever think so. She was so sophisticated she might have been two years older and her mode of dress was the height of fashion. She was a very nice person and had a good job. My brother Peter became very friendly with her for a time. I think Peter had started his training at Greenwich Royal Naval College about this time because he had managed to get a commission, but I can't remember seeing him while I was in London though I may have done.

I did see Mother a few times, but they were few and far between. I know I had to rely on Mother to be a guarantor for me when I needed a lot of fillings to all my top front teeth, The dentist having examined my teeth would not treat me without a letter from Mother to say he would be paid. I think she was teaching somewhere where she was living in and I know the account came to over six pounds, which was a great deal of money when my wages were only ten shillings each week. The dentist certainly was paid and I think Mother either helped or lent me the money until 1 had saved enough.

While I was at Bayswater I used to see various newspapers, though I didn't buy them. On one occasion I was looking at the Evening News when I came across a very small paragraph stating that a small plane had crashed but the two occupants were not seriously hurt and their names were given. One of them was Sally's. 1 knew he sometimes flew planes. Some years later I was told that at a later date he had been killed while flying. It was not anything to do with the war. In fact I am almost sure it was before the war and it must have been Peter who told me, as he would have been told by Mary.

Plate Titles

Section Six

37) 1936. Thea and Ray.

38) 1936? Cook and chauffeur at Monkton Wyld Court.

39) 1936. Me on Timhorse.

40) 1936. Sandy on Timhorse with me.

41) 1936. Biddy.

42) 1936. A puppy with the railway crriage used as sleeping quarters.

43) 1936. Francis and Anthea at Monkton Wyld.

44) 1936. Michael on Timhorse.

45) 1936. Michael on Kitty.

46) 1936. Michael on Kitty.

47) 1936. Michael's Popdog.

48) 1937. Ray and Thea atop with others plus Fursey sitting on the running board of the Austin parked by the stables.

49) 1937. Michael holding Popdog and Robin.

50) 1937. Prince.

51) 1937. Monkton Wyld Court showing the skylight in the nursery.

52) Late thirties. Mum and Dad.

CHAPTER IX

MONKTON WYLD COURT

In May of 1937 1 went to Monkton Wyld Court again at Wendy's request. I was there for the next three years. I can't say I left London never to return, but certainly never to return for any length of time. I said my good byes' to Mater but I did visit her later. There were also times when 1 went to see Mother first in one flat and then another in Winchmore Hill where she lived near to where she was teaching. Rather like we used to do at home, we changed some of the rooms round from time to time and people slept in various places.

When I arrived that year Wendy was expecting her second baby. Francis was by then almost three and Anthea who was just three was still there. 1 am not sure who had been looking after them, but it was from then my place to do so. Wendy and Geoffrey were at that time sleeping in the room that had been the bar the previous year. It was just to the right as one entered the front door. I slept at first with the children in the nursery, sometimes I had a small narrow bed in there, at others, a large double bed. At times I slept in the bedroom opposite the nursery, at others in the bedroom next to the nursery. Later on I slept over the stables, and at another time in the annexe. Before I slept there though, the annexe had been let to various people.

In the paddock where there were two cows and at times some of the horses, there was what had once been a railway carriage. I didn't ever sleep in it but it made a useful extra place for various members of staff to have their own bedrooms. Because of all the moving about it is not possible to remember just where everyone slept, or when they moved into different places. Obviously the main house had guests in all the bedrooms, and there were fourteen, in the summer months. During the winter some had guests in and others had various members of staff. Whereas when I had been there the year before, there was a cook her husband was a chauffeur handyman, though not very handy I gathered, and there was a dinning room maid by the time 1 came again they had all gone. They had been the old-fashioned servant variety. In their place was another cook who had a rather useless daughter aged about fourteen who just stayed there and did as she liked. They were not there for long but I remember being really furious with this cook over something to do with her daughter and told her what I thought in no uncertain words. I am not given to seeing red as a rule, so although I forget the exact reason, I do remember the occasion. I was in the kitchen at the time and it stands out like a sore thumb! At first there were not many staff so Geoffrey tried to do no end of things including waiting at tables. I am not sure if my sister Dorothea was still there as housekeeper. I think she may have been as Ray who was engaged to her, visited her at times. We later had a Mrs Struthers whom we all called Peter. She had a boy aged nine called John. He was one of my charges. My Father was there most of the time that I was, but I don't remember if he was already there by the time I came for the second time.

About six weeks after I arrived Wendy went into Axminster Cottage Hospital and two weeks later returned with her daughter Helen. She was a very beautiful baby who looked more like two months than two weeks. Although Wendy had her in a crib in their room for a few weeks she was soon given into my charge, with a few special instructions from Wendy but mostly I was given complete charge of her and enjoyed the responsibility. My hospital training served me in good stead and I was very particular about how I coped. She needed very little attention beyond the usual basics, as she never cried, though she had done a little during the evening, when she first came from the hospital and Wendy was feeding her. After her bath and ten o'clock feed in the morning she went out in the pram on the terrace under the shade of a tree and was content asleep or awake until the next feed at two o'clock. Wendy by then had taken on the cooking and had very little time for the baby or the other children. She once made the remark that she didn't ever hear Helen cry and wanted to know if she ever did and also wanted to know if she was all right. I was able to assure her that she was a model baby by day and night and frequently played with her toes and 'talked' happily to the branches of the tree above her when she was in her pram. Later when the weather was not so good, or if it rained the pram was put under cover in the courtyard outside the dairy window, where she was just as happy. Just sometimes I was asked to fetch her for Wendy, and Geoffrey if he was about, so that they could see her. She was always a good placid baby with plenty of smiles on these occasions. During the height of the summer season I was at times taken by car with about five children aged between three and five to The Cobb at Lyme Regis, for a couple of hours during the afternoon for them to enjoy the sands and a paddle in the sea. It was usually Geoffrey who took us and returned to pick us up later. As Helen was left in her pram during that time Wendy would always say she would keep an eye on her. She may have sometimes asked someone to just look to see if she was all right. I doubt if she ever looked at her herself, knowing Wendy. They had a very intelligent mongrel dog, who took it upon herself to guard the baby when she was in her pram. Biddy slept under the pram while it was outside and had there been anything amiss she would soon have let the world know.

The children I took to the sea belonged to various guests. Guests were always told they could leave their children with me anytime they liked and some of them did from time to time and some often did most of the time they were staying there. Sometimes I just had charge of them in the garden or while having their meals and ages varied from three to thirteen. Miss Harvey who had rented the annex the year before had gone to live in the New Forest. Lesley, who was her companion help, frequently came to Monkton Wyld Court and was eventually almost permanently there. She became godMother to

Helen the baby who, I think was so called because Lesley had wished her to be called after Miss Harvey whose name was Helen.

One summer the M.P. Quentin Hogg, who later became Lord Chancellor of the Exchequer, Lord Hailsham, rented the annexe for his family for their holidays. He very often came down to the house and sat in the kitchen drinking cups of tea while chatting to Wendy. I often made the tea and stood leaning against the second table that was by the window listening and drinking tea also! I don't think I ever followed what was said. It was all politics, but I was not the only one that was there drinking cups of tea most times. We did see his wife and family but only very rarely.

Wendy's parents sometimes came and so did Geoffrey's. Those would also be times when I would be asked to bring the baby and of course Francis for them to see. Wendy had twin sisters. I had met them years before when I first met Wendy. One of them came with her husband once while I was there. Geoffrey had a brother. He and his wife came a number of times with their two small sons. I usually had them to care for when they came. When the elder of the two was about five or six, he had to be operated on for a brain tumour. Fortunately he made a complete recovery.

Wendy and Geoffrey had the best bedroom that was near the bathroom on the first landing during the winter, but later on there was a large hut built outside in which they slept. Sandy was one of the people who slept at times in one of the railway carriage rooms. Others slept there too but I am hot sure who, as we had so many who came just for a short time. Sandy who was Miss Marjory Sanders was always called Sandy and was known as the lady gardener. I suppose it was not very usual to have a gardener who was a lady but Sandy had been to a horticultural college so was very knowledgeable. Furzey had done the garden at first but Sandy must have come soon after I had been there the first time, and then took charge of the garden. One reason not to use her first name may have been because although Wendy was never called by her first name except by her parents, she too was Marjory. As Furzey lived locally and came daily, he didn't come at the weekends. That meant that someone had to milk the cows then. Sandy found herself doing this and I know there were a few occasions when either Wendy or Geoffrey did so but quite a few others learned to and helped out. I know I was one who did and I think Dorothea did too. Sandy had a young man to help her for a while but I don't think he was there long. Then she had Ann, another young lady who had been to college. There was a very large walled garden to manage as well as the rest of the garden which was far too much for one. Furzey did a lot of the rough work like scything the long rough grass at the bottom of the garden above the field, and probably in the orchard. I expect he did some digging amongst other things or whatever Sandy asked of him. He came on a bicycle and brought his lunch each day. Coming and going at regular times. Sandy worked all hours when necessary and joined in a lot of the fun as well, as did all of us. Sandy managed to produce all kinds of things from the garden. She kept the house supplied with as many vegetables as were wanted no matter how many guests there were. From potatoes to asparagus, artichokes both globe and Jerusalem, runner beans and tomatoes, lettuces, cucumber, marrow's, various fruit and other things I can't think of. There was always plenty to do.

Mrs Blanchard was a friend of Wendy's from when they had lived in Surrey. They had been friends for a long time but because Francis couldn't say Blanchard when he was about two, he called her Buntub and it stuck forever after. We all called her 'Buntub' for evermore. She must have been in her late fifties when she came and was a widow. She had a son John who was in his thirties and very much a bachelor. He visited from time to time but he had a good job in London or Surrey where he lived. When Buntub first came she helped clean bedrooms but later on she helped with all kinds of things as and when she thought fit. If she was about and I needed someone to hold the baby for a few minutes she was always pleased to oblige and more than once she remarked that she liked to hold the baby because she always smelt nice. She was often the one to make the tea at any time of day as Wendy drank cups of tea all day long. Wendy had goats and Buntub would go out with Wendy to help to see to them. Later on Buntub almost took charge of the goats as, in later years they were taken for walks and would follow Buntub. She was a little person with grey hair worn in a plait round her head. Inclined to be a little shy so was never keen to join in any fun times, but Wendy could persuade almost anyone to do anything she wanted them to so Buntub didn't get out of joining in everything. She was also a bit old fashioned but everyone always liked her. Although I looked after the children, I was also one of many who waited at table in the evening which was after the children were in bed. The dinning room had been moved to one that was nearer to the kitchen. It had two doors, one near a door that led on to the terrace in the garden that the guests used, and another that was a swing door near the bottom of the back stairs which had a door through which one had to go in order to go up them. The swing door came into the passage that went past the pantry and along to the kitchen. When waiting at table it was very handy to be able to open the door by walking backwards into it when holding at least three plates, or a tray full of any number. With instructions from Wendy I soon mastered the art of waiting at table!

Wendy was good with her sewing machine and made an overall of pink denim for me to wear by day when with the children and a number of blue flowery cotton overalls for anyone who was waiting at table to wear while doing so, They had short sleeves and a collar and wrapped over like a coat to button up with loops in the front. They were fairly long and there were several sizes.

During the summer holidays we had university students to help out with anything they were asked to do. One very good looking and well liked one was Peter who took on all the washing up from the dinning room in the pantry. There was one lady in her eighties who was named Zoe Hawley. We always politely addressed her as Miss Hawley but she was always spoken of as Zoe. She occupied the very largest bedroom on the first floor , which was immediately below the nursery and above the lounge with the anti room that adjoined it. The latter had a wash basin in it and was her bedroom. The large room was her sitting room. She had been a suffragette and was a little eccentric. She was a law unto herself. She had a little grey cairndog called Winkle. She did a lot of walking and took Winkle with her. She was only in residence during the summer returning to her hotel in London during the winter but the rooms were rented by her all the year round.

It was one of Buntub's jobs to take her morning tea into her and see to her bed and rooms. No one else was allowed in there as a rule. She liked to do some gardening so became friendly with Sandy and remained so to the end of her days. I think she lived to be ninety six. She also drove a small car very badly but she had never had to take a test as those who could drive before tests became compulsory in 1934 didn't have to take a test. On one occasion she "commanded' a local bobby to send a whole line of traffic back so that she could drive through where single line traffic was indicated. She had the kind of voice that no one ever dared to contradict and he did as he was bid. At the age of eighty-one she rode a pony for the first time in her life under Wendy's tuition. I don't think she did it twice though. Her own meals were individually cooked to her order. She had to have brains cooked in milk in the oven one-day and sweetbreads another and so on. Tea was always China without milk. Her toast was always melba toast. Very thin slices of white bread, baked to a light golden brown in the oven and woe betide anyone who let the tiniest bit of it burn because it would be useless to send it into her, she would soon send it back, so one had to start all over again. She also had to have a junket made for her everyday and lettuce served at lunchtime with whatever she had. We were never quite sure whether the junket was for her or for Winkle. Every week a cod's head was ordered for her from the fishmonger. This had to be boiled and put on a dish in the larder to cool. Before her own evening meal she would ask for the cod's head to be brought into the pantry where she took some of the flesh from the bones to give to Winkle with some dog biscuit. She left the dish in the pantry and it was returned to the cool larder to be covered and kept for the next day. There were no refrigerators in those days. One day when Peter was in the pantry he found the dish of what was left of the cod's head. He knew nothing of Zoe feeding Winkle from it and assuming it was finished with diligently cleared it away by throwing it into the bucket where the tealeaves were always put. Zoe came in asking where Winkle's cod's head was saying that it should be on a dish for her. Peter suddenly cottoned on to what he had done and asked if what he had thrown away was what she was looking for. It was of course. "Pray take it out young man" she said and Peter although completely flummoxed, being the charming young man that he was, replied, "Certainly mam," and proceeded to get as much of the cod's head as he possibly could from amongst the tealeaves with his bare hands!

Many people came as guests because they liked the idea of being able to have a ride on a horse. Wendy and Geoffrey both rode well. They had about five horses. One was a pony suitable for children to ride and the first time I rode it I managed to fall off and hurt my back. Fortunately not very seriously. There was one light chestnut mare that was very placid and easy to ride called Diana. I rode her a few times. There was another smaller one called Gold. I liked riding her. There was Tim that no one could ever be sure of so at that time I didn't usually try him and there was a very large dark bay called Nimrod. My younger brother Michael came to Monkton Wyld Court when he left school and he spent most of his time with the horses. It didn't take him long to learn to ride, and he did fall off Tim at times, he once told me, mostly in the paddock but he didn't tell people or let anyone know in case they stopped him riding. There were large fields about a mile away where the horses were most of the time when they were not being ridden, but sometimes one or more of them were in the paddock which was handy when they were wanted.

When one year Wendy and Geoffrey went to the auctions on Exmore for the wild ponies they brought one back which they called Prince. He was a very beautiful slim black pony, completely wild. Michael tamed and trained him to do just what he wanted, by talking to him. It was all done by kindness Michael had a way with animals, particularly horses and all children loved him. He was very good with them no matter how small. He had one of the puppies that were born to a bitch that had got out at the wrong time. Pop was its name and often called Popdog. A very small black dog that he trained to leap up into his arms when he told it to. By the time Michael was seventeen he had been riding sometime and had been jumping Nimrod. When there was a county show at Axminster, he and Nimrod were entered to jump. It was a great shame that because Nimrod was not used to an audience he refused to jump at all in the ring. Michael then took him straight to the practice enclosure where there was no audience and Nimrod jumped as well as he always did. It was not long after that, that Michael took a teaching job for a short while and when he was old enough he applied to go into the cavalry. They had no vacancies so he went into the Fleet Air Arm. While still at Monkton Wyld Court he had been riding with the local hunt, unofficially more than once and thoroughly enjoyed it. He was really keen on horses and so good with them. He said his ambition was to run riding stables.

I had not been at Monkton Wyld Court long when Winifred and Lewis visited us. They were living in Devon in the bungalow where we had stayed nearly two years before. They brought their son John with them. He had been born in May and was by then a very big baby aged three months. They were calling in as they passed on their way to somewhere else. I am not sure if they lived anywhere before going to Woking but they were certainly at Woking later on where Winifred had a teaching job.

During the summer while there were plenty of guests. Wendy and Geoffrey spent quite a number of evenings entertaining them with music and sketches. Wendy played the piano and Geoffrey had a very good tenor voice. He was also a good actor. Sometimes other members of staff were cajoled into joining in and doing a bit of performing. Most people wore long evening dresses on these occasions. I didn't have any long dresses so Wendy passed on two to me. One had a square neck and puffed sleeves. It was made of linen and was covered with a pink floral design backed with an off white colour. I wore it a lot because I liked it so much. More than ten years later I made a child's dress out of it for my daughter. The other was black. It had no sleeves and a V-neck line both front and back. It was lined and had alternate bands of lace and velvet over the lining. It must have been very expensive in the first place as it had been Wendy's Mother's, and she was the sort of person who could afford to and did go to the best fashion houses. I still have it!

During these evenings one of Geoffrey's favourite sketches was, "I've a hole in my bucket." and he dressed to suit the part. In the kitchen were two AGA cookers. These needed to be stoked and filled at twelve-hour intervals. As the morning stoking was done soon after breakfast the evening stoking needed to be done at about ten o'clock, when the entertainment was in full swing. It was

Geoffrey who did this job as a rule. Of course I had to offer to do it for him, going out into the kitchen in my evening dress to stoke the AGAS. After that I often did them and later even in the morning when the ashes needed to be taken away. On the wall in the kitchen was a set of bells each with a bedroom number on and others for the lounge and dinning room and so on. They were not rung often but had to be answered if they were, I didn't do that as a rule, but you may depend on it Zoe rang hers at times. The first time I went to Monkton Wyld, the opera The Jolly Roger had just been performed in Axminster. Wendy was the conductor and Geoffrey took the tenor lead. Later on it was The Chocolate Soldier. I was roped in to join in. Never mind that I couldn't sing, dance or act. It was no use protesting. Wendy was conducting and if she told you that you could, you just did! We met a lot of the local people at rehearsals. Wendy told me that my voice was mezzo-soprano, which I had never heard of before. I had a not so young rather rotund man as a partner for dancing and I actually sang one line solo! It was really great fun so in the end I thoroughly enjoyed it.

Another thing Wendy undertook was to form a choir. It was amazing the way she made everyone sing, We did the Messiah. It was an experience I wouldn't have missed for anything. We had Margaret Ritchie taking the lead and Geoffrey the tenor lead. I forget who the contralto was but Harry Echevereer sang the bass. He was an English speaking Spanish blind man. We got to know him and Margaret Ritchie quite well. Later When Michael was no longer able to have his Popdog Harry agreed to take him for Michael as he had been quite attached to the little dog.

The first Autumn I was there Wendy thought it would be useful it I could learn to drive. I was given every opportunity to go in the car whenever shopping had to be done and at other times as long as the children were not in the car, They had two cars. One was an Austin sixteen. This was the one I drove at first. I was even allowed to practise on my own in the drive because there was plenty of room to come from the garage to the front door where there was turning space and it gave me plenty of practice in reversing. I took my first test in Dorchester in December 1937. Although I had been doing well, I was so nervous I couldn't get it right. One only had to wait one month after a test to take another so the next one was in Exeter in January 1938. 1 took a third also in Exeter in February and failed them both. At that age sitting in a car next to a strange man was, I found too disconcerting for words. However, Wendy and Geoffrey refused to let me give up and in March in Dorchester again I passed. I remember so well Geoffrey saying to me when he saw the examiner, "Well at least he is a gentleman, he is wearing suede shoes so you'll be all right this time!" From then on I often found myself doing the shopping. Biddy liked to go in the car whenever she could. When she heard the word car she would find her way to it and sit by it until someone came to drive it. During the winter I had a long navy blue coat which I wore when going in the car. If Biddy saw me put it on she followed me until I went to the car. At times for fun, I played a game with her by shutting the door at the bottom of the back stairs leaving her the other side of it. Quick as a flash she would go round the other way to find me, usually before 1 got to the car. But I would never leave her behind it I could help it. When I was shopping she was too useful. She sat on the back seat and didn't expect to get out once we were parked in the square in Axminster and one never needed to lock the door of the car as Biddy was an excellent guard dog. One day the man in the shop had put a box of groceries in the car as he usually did and then realised he had put the wrong box in. Biddy never took any notice of anyone who put anything into the car but when the man went to retrieve the wrong box Biddy got up and growled at him. No way was she going to let him have it so he had to wait for whoever was driving to return before he could exchange the wrong box for the correct one. I don't know who was driving that time as quite a number of people drove at different times. When I had been learning to drive although it was mostly Geoffrey who came with me and taught me, sometimes it was Wendy or at other times someone called Sheila who spent most of her time helping in the kitchen or washing up or preparing vegetables in the scullery. She was nearer thirty than twenty. Another person who helped me by sitting with me when I was learning was Vera Kantrovich, a well-known violinist at that time. She stayed with us for quite a while and played in the orchestra when we performed Messiah. She had a three-year-old son who was most of the time with the other children. Vera helped in the house in various ways, probably dusting or cleaning. We were all rather like one big family. Everyone called Wendy 'Mummie' and Geoffrey 'Daddy.' No end of people took a hand in, doing all kinds of things. Michael helped by polishing the floors with a heavy buffer on the end of a long handle and he did other things at times too. So many things happened during the three years that I was at Monkton Wyld that I can't remember the correct sequence of events. A journalist came one day to interview Wendy with the idea of giving the guesthouse a write up in a catering magazine. He made a terrific job of it, a lot of it was grossly exaggerated and he had a full two-page article as a result. A lot of us had a good laugh about it when we saw it!

Peter was at the Royal Naval College in Greenwich during this time and had taken a fancy to Sally's sister Mary. When at the end of his time a dinner and dance was held, he invited Mary and I managed to get him to say I could come too. Wendy let me borrow the car. I went first to Kensington, where Mary lived with Mater as she had said I could stay the night. By then I had a puppy. It had fairly long hair and was nearly all black. It was half sister to Michael's Popdog. I took her with me and after changing left her in the bedroom where I was to sleep with Mary while we went to the dinner and dance. I did enjoy it most of the evening but when it came to the last dance I felt rather like a fish out of water, and stood there like a lemon. Peter had Mary for a partner and I didn't have one! When we returned to Mater's I found my dog Toni had chewed the belt of my nice Chinese Kimono that Peter had brought back from China and given to me. The next day I went to stay the night with Mother at her flat. Actually it was the first of two flats Mother lived in when she was teaching at a day school in Winchmore Hill. The address was 35 Queen's Avenue, which I mention because years later, we laughed when we found our address was 35 Queen's Avenue in Dorchester! The flat was rather small and on the first floor. Sylvia came while I was there. The flat at the top of the house was empty and they were able to borrow a camp bed for me to sleep on in an otherwise empty room at the top of the house. When I started to go back to Monkton Wyld, at about six in the evening. I lost my way trying to get out of London. One hour later I found I had gone round in a circle and was about a mile from where I had started out. It was ten to midnight when, because I had not allowed for going round in a circle in

London. I ran out of petrol half way up Chideock Hill. For anyone who doesn't know, it is long and very steep and it was pitch black at the time, but there was no traffic about. I was most fortunate though because there was one lone petrol pump at the bottom of the hill. I couldn't see to back down, there were no white lines or cat eyes, so I left Toni in the car and walked down to knock at the door of the cottage where the pump was. An old man put his head out of the window. He was wearing a nightcap! When he heard of my plight, he very kindly came down to fill a gallon can with petrol. I paid him for the petrol and he lent me the can trusting me to return it to his step when I had put the petrol in the car. When I arrived back Lesley was waiting up for me to make sure I was all right as they had expected me to be back much earlier.

Dear, kind Lesley, she would do almost anything for anybody. When I was doing other things it was mostly she who took charge of the children. At one time when Helen was past the stage of spending most of her day in the pram. I had a girl to help me. She was not much younger than I was, and was quite good with the children. She didn't mind doing any of the cleaning that was involved to do with the children. That let me out of the sort of chores I was not keen on. Anthea had gone by then but there was a little boy much the same age as Helen. His parents were in Australia. His name was Christopher but the nearest he could get to that was 'Digger' so that was as often as not what he was called. Francis had a few unusual words besides Buntub for Blanchard. He would talk about a hottle wattle bottle as Wendy often had one, and he called himself 'Buffines', so he was often called that when he was quite small.

There were always at least two cars and for a time a van. One of the cars was an Armstrong Siddeley. It had a pre-selected gear lever on the steering wheel column. It was quite easy to drive. It had been passed on to Wendy by her father, At one time there was a dark blue Austin twelve and later on a rather sleek looking silver coloured car, that we always referred to as the "Silver Bullet"'. I drove them all in turn and learned how to change a wheel and sometimes cope with a carburettor that didn't always do what it should. They had a trailer that I took to the store near the station in Axminster where animal feed was sold. I sometimes had to hitch or unhitch the trailer in order to turn it round if turning space was limited, and more than once huge bags of animal feed were left out on a platform to be collected after the store was closed and I humped the bags into the trailer to bring them back, about four or five different kinds of food for horses, goats, cows and pigs. They had pigs too. There were pens in the paddock where the cows were milked, that housed pigs at times and goats at other times, too. Sometimes I used the van for collecting feed, or for shopping. One day I had Lesley with me when, as I came round a corner something was parked on the other side of the road and a car was coming down the road towards me. The van came to a halt when I braked suddenly in the ditch. We were not hurt or even very shaken but the van was then useless. I gathered after that the back axle had previously been bent so it was not surprising that it became useless. In order to get the car or the van started there were many times when they had to be cranked with a handle that was fitted in the front of the vehicle and taken out once the engine was working. Care had to be taken as it could kick back as it fired and if you were not ready for it an arm could be broken. I did this cranking quite a number of times but fortunately kept my arm intact! Another vehicle that I tried one time was a motorcycle and sidecar that Geoffrey had. I tried it just once in the drive where there was plenty of room, but all it did was steer into the bank at the side of the drive so I didn't try it again.

In addition to learning to milk the cows and the goats, I learned to make clotted cream from the cow's milk and small quantities of butter with an ordinary hand egg whisk. When the butter was made it had to be salted and the whey that was left made the most delicious bread if it was mixed with white self raising flour and put into a very hot oven. The goats milk if left to go sour we made into lovely cheese by putting it into a cloth and hanging it up. I think it sometimes had to have an addition to help it sour and the whey from that was not used but the cheese really tasted good. There were plenty of chickens so there were always plenty of eggs and by Christmas there were cockerels to be plucked. They had to be slaughtered first so as at that time I would try almost anything. I soon learned how to wring a cockerel's neck correctly but I couldn't do that now.

There were two beehives in the Annexe garden. Geoffrey dressed in suitable gear of special thick gloves and hat that had a net coming down over his face and at the back of his neck dealt with them and produced honey from them. Sandy was once stung by a bee and not only had a very swollen arm as a result but was very ill for some days. On one occasion the bees swarmed. They were on a fairly low branch of a tree. The idea was to shake the branch of the tree so that they would drop into a skep which is a very large bowl shaped wicker basket. Geoffrey had his gear on and who do you think volunteered to hold the skep? I had not imagined how heavy it would be so of course, as they fell I dropped it. There were plenty of people about watching. I don't remember who shook the branch just that Geoffrey was standing by to take the skep from me and all he got was an empty one. The bees had gone. I think they were retrieved later but without my help I was not stung and I don't remember whether anyone else was or not.

Many of the guests I don't recall at all but quite a few I particularly remember for certain reasons. There was Mrs Bubb who had two Samoyed dogs. They are white dogs with very thick coats from the Arctic originally. They are intended to pull sledges but all hers ever pulled was Mrs Bubb herself . She had quite a job to hold on to them. She was with us sometime and she kept her dogs in her bedroom. It was not unusual for one to escape. She spent a lot of time grooming them and then made the hair into yarn that she could knit into garments.

Titus was a young man I thought I fancied but I ran and hid as soon as he made any advances in my direction so that came to nothing but he wasn't with us very long and while he was, he spent some time in bed because he was ill, so he had to be waited on in his bedroom. I did have a post card from him after he left in November 1938 from Latvia near Russia. Pinto was a character, not easy to describe. He was a bachelor in his fifties and liked long discussions of the academic type with Wendy. Sometimes he was with us for quite a time then he would go and come again. He made trips abroad sometimes and sent post cards to some of us. His full name was Pintolete but he was always called Pinto. However, his signature was unique. Because I collected post cards I still have one from him sent from Beaminster with his signature. It is a funny little thin running man with a line across the top of it. It is dated August 1939. He was an artist of sorts, but more of a writer, not that he needed to be as he was a man of means. He told us that he went to bed early so that he could have about three hours sleep and then spend a couple of hours writing while it was quiet in the middle of the night and then have some more sleep. He often went for solitary walks. One day when I was at the fields where the goats and horses were kept, I was on my own and as was usual there was no one about. Pinto turned up and we stood chatting near a gate. Suddenly and quite unexpectedly, he tried, not very successfully to kiss me. I was amazed but to give him his due when he realised he had made a faux pas he apologised and we forgot it so to speak. Although I was horrified at the time. I laughed about it later! He was in fact a gentleman. Rumour had it that he was a count but I am not sure how much truth there was in that.

Another 1938 Post card I have is addressed to Maureen. It is a picture of Snow White and her forest friends. Maureen was a three-year-old who had a brother who was five. They were two of five children I used to have on the sands at The Cobb in Lyme Regis. Francis and another boy called Iain who was four and Anthea made the five. I was waiting for the car to fetch us one day when a complete stranger asked if they were quins. I assured him they were not and that none of them were mine.

One year when there was snow on the ground, several of us went with Geoffrey to the fields to round up the horses and give them hay. There was a large haystack in the barn. The hay had not been made into bales and the bales stacked. It was one very large stack. Hay had to be cut from it with a very large knife made for the purpose. The blade was about six or seven inches wide and several feet long from the handle through which one put four fingers, to the end where it tapered slightly. Large chunks the size of a bale could be cut from the stack with it and the hay then fed to the horses. I learned to do this so that when I went up to the fields alone which I sometimes did. I could cope. The time the snow was on the ground and we had finished feeding the horses and returned to the Guest House Geoffrey found he had lost his watch. Fortunately it was a waterproof one. We returned to the field where we had been and retraced our steps in a line across the field searching as we went. Someone spotted it half way across. There was one weekend when we had what became known as the three haymakers. It was haymaking time. It was done with a pitchfork, a rake, and a lorry to take the load and many helpers. I was one of the helpers part of the time. The three young men who were there for just one long week end were from London. All three in business of some kind and one was married. I spent one evening with each of them in turn and none of them were very pleased when they found I was not prepared to give them what they considered was 'a good time'. With anyone I had only just met kisses were all they got from me. One had taken me out in his car and said when he realised the position. "0h, you're a good girl, are you?" "Afraid so", I replied and he then drove back!

Wendy had more and more goats, so she took quite a number of them to the County Agricultural Show at Axminster. This was not very long before Miles was born. Of course Geoffrey went with her and was there most of the time as someone had to sleep at the show for the night with the goats in case anyone interfered with them. I think she had a few rosettes for her trouble but I don't remember how many. As all sorts of people used to help with all sorts of things. I have no idea who did the cooking at that time. Miles was born at the beginning of September 1938, a little prematurely which was not to be wondered at when one thought about how Wendy spent her time with goats and many other things. He was therefore rather small when born but not all that small. He was not placid like his sister Helen had been but in no time he thrived on goat's milk mainly under my care. I became his godMother.

Later on I did quite a lot of cooking not that I knew much about it at first, but with Wendy to tell you what to do it was quite easy to learn, and at that time I quite enjoyed it.

During the winter of 1938 I undertook a lot of decorating. It was the same old story. Wendy said some of the bedrooms needed to be decorated and as usual I said, "I'll do it." After that I went to bed fairly early each evening. I was sleeping in the room near the front door at the time. If I left the window open Biddy would jump in and sleep on my bed. At first my Father who was always up early, brought me a cup of tea at half past five. I then had two hours in which to put wallpamure on the walls of the bedrooms. After a time I didn't need a shout and in the end did seven of the bedrooms. Some had sloping walls that went almost to a peak at the top. Some were very high and I had a small pair of quite easy to manage steps, which I put on top of a very sturdy table to reach the top in some rooms. It was an oilbound distemper I was using which was very easy to stir and use. The rooms were all done in a cream colour. I found it good fun to do.

My Father usually sat in the kitchen drinking his cups of tea from early in the morning. As people gravitated to the kitchen he would have tea for them. Sandy who was a fairly early riser was one of the first, and told me she had many interesting conversations with him.

Soon after that Wendy wanted to experiment with special feeding stuffs for the goats to improve them and their milk yield. My Father who had a chemistry degree was asked by her to be the analytical chemist for the herd and he spent hours mixing and analysing goat food with of course a promise of payment, which he told me later he never did receive. Wendy often lived in a dream world and imagined she could make her goats better than anyone else. The result of the special food was enormous kids. The poor goats had a very difficult time giving birth because of the size of the kids. A few of us took it in turns to stay with the goats that were having trouble, all night. I was only one of a number to stay up and help. Then one morning after an all night session 1 found I was covered in a rash. It was German measles. I was then isolated in a spare bedroom until I was no longer infectious. Sandy was one of the people who brought food to me while I was there on my own. One day she brought me a chunk of cheese, thinking I would like it. As a small child I disliked it intensely and never ate it. As this cheese had been brought into the sick room I couldn't send it away for anyone else to eat. I was still of the opinion that food must never be wasted. I struggled through that cheese and with great difficulty finished it. I can't say I enjoyed it but from then on I have from time to time eaten cheese, and now quite like it.

They had their own billy goat for the nanny goats. He smelt horrible particularly during the winter, which was the rutting season. He lived in the orchard in his own special wooden hut and was tethered on a long strong chain with a swivel attached so that he couldn't get tangled. In spite of that he sometimes managed to get loose and usually ate the orchard hedges. One day he was found eating the flowers round the war memorial near the church. He was so strong that only a bucket of dry food would entice him back to where he belonged and even that was quite difficult to achieve, it usually took two of us. He was fed twice each day with a net full of hay and some mixed dry food. He was sometimes tethered on a stake away from his hut but in the orchard to eat whatever he fancied. He also had to have a fresh bucket of water each day. Contrary to common belief the goats did not eat just anything. They would nibble at all kinds of things then drop or leave it if it didn't suit them and most things did not except the most choice of tit bits or their own special food. They ate bread but not if it had been dropped on the floor and picked up again. As with most things it was Geoffrey's job to feed the billy and that meant that I frequently did. A special coat had to be worn because once the billy had rubbed against you it was almost if not quite impossible to get the smell out of your clothes. I would do almost anything for Geoffrey by then. I suppose I sort of hero worshipped him, As I have said a lot of us called Wendy and Geoffrey Mummy and Daddy and 1 thought of Geoffrey rather as a second Daddy. He was a very kind loving man and I became very fond of him. Before going to bed if I could get a goodnight hug and kiss from him, which I often did, it made my day.

In the cow sheds in the paddock there were pens with pigs and their piglets in. Furzey usually fed them except at the weekends. Then someone else had to, When they were big enough to be sold I took some to market in the trailer to be auctioned. They didn't fetch as good a price as they might have done so when the next ones were ready, Wendy asked the butcher if he was interested. He was, so it was arranged for him to come and look and make an offer. Wendy said she didn't think he would offer what she thought we ought to get. I say 'we' because of course I offered to take him down the paddock to see them and said that if Wendy would leave it to me I would get a good price. She agreed to this and I then asked what the very minimum was that she would accept. I don't remember the prices but I do remember being more than successful by insisting that I knew Wendy wouldn't let them go for less than a certain price and bargaining with him. Finally I said I thought his last offer might be acceptable and I would go and ask. I went into the house. I didn't need to ask as it was more than Wendy had said they were worth in the first place. The butcher came and took them. I was very pleased to help him load them into his van. There were lambs that came from a nearby farm. Any lambs that were orphaned or if a sheep had three lambs and could only manage two, or other surplus lambs, we had to bottle feed. We fed them on goat's milk and they thrived. It was great fun while it lasted, which was not for very long but I became really skilled at holding no less than five bottles at one time. There were quite a lot of lambs sometimes and although there were others to help with the feeding at times. I often needed to cope with as many as possible as they all wanted to feed at once. I could put one bottle in between my knees and then hold two in each hand. Later they went in the fields that were a mile or so up the road and had grass and hay. They became enormous. This was not quite such a good idea as it sounded though. When we asked the butcher to look at them and make an offer. He said he couldn't give us lamb prices which were much more than mutton prices, because although he said he did believe me when I told him how young they were he could not offer them to his customers as lamb. They would not buy at the price. There was no bargaining at all possible. It was his offer or nothing.

There were at times quite a lot of kids to bottle feed too. They were not left with their Mothers for long as the goats had to be milked to keep up the yield and some of them gave huge quantities. For a time there was a milk round to do in Axminster. I did it a few times. I used Kitty the pony with a trap to take the milk round. Kitty was a very sturdy pony that could safely he ridden by children, or used with the trap, She was easy to drive except that when we were on the way home, she knew it and was a job to hold on to as she rushed along the lanes taking corners rather more sharply than she should. Once it was wartime and there was very little petrol, Kitty was most useful as she could be used for shopping of all kind. Prince the pony that Michael had trained so well was sold to the butcher. He was a very kind man and wanted it for his seven-year-old daughter. Unfortunately there was a terrible accident when the child was standing outside the butchers shop. It was by then wartime and an army vehicle backed into her. She was killed outright. I imagine the butcher sold Prince but we never heard anything about him.

Most of the time when I was doing other things Lesley took over looking after the children but other people did too. Lesley also did all kinds of things. It was quite usual for almost anyone to do anything at Wendy's request, whether staff or guest. Wendy often took to her bed when she thought she would and Lesley was good at massaging her aches and pains away even if she didn't have any! Geoffrey was ill at one time and I took my turn to take tea or food to him and make the bed. Wendy sometimes had a meal in bed but she almost lived on cups of tea. They both had drinks at times but not all that often. They introduced me to dry sherry, which I enjoyed on occasion but it was not partaken by anyone to any extent.

Another thing I had a lot to do with were the accounts. For a long time almost nothing was done about them. It was Geoffrey's province and he didn't like doing them at all. "Show me what you want done, and I'll do it if you like," I said. From then on I sorted invoices and accounts and even got to the point where Wendy got me to sign her cheques for her. When the phone went I answered it saying that it was the secretary speaking! Wendy was frequently 'not at home' even if she was sitting in the kitchen and I had to take a message if possible. I got to know so much about the business that I could often give an answer to whatever was wanted.

In the simmer of 1939 with war imminent there were very few guests and no extra children to look after. I now have no idea why but I, for some obscure reason became very morose. I was sent off up to London to stay for a couple of weeks with Mater. I returned on the eve of the day war was declared. With no money and no ticket, the stationmaster at Waterloo allowed me to travel by train after Wendy or Geoffrey had been in touch promising that my fare would be paid. I was handed over, so to speak, to Sandy, who kindly took me under her wing and had me digging in the garden. I was hopeless at digging but I suppose it did me good. I was soon back to my old self!

That winter we had what were known as 'village hops' in the church hall run by the vicar's daughter. We also had keep fit classes that we attended. They too were run by the vicar's daughter. In Lyme Regis they needed volunteers to make sandwiches for the troops and to serve cups of tea in a canteen. Several of us went to do that a few evenings each week. Francis was by then five years old. Geoffrey wanted him to have some lessons. I said I didn't think I could cope with teaching just one child on his own. I don't remember who took it on, probably Lesley, but later on I had a hand in teaching him. The goats still had to be milked, and kids fed. They were in the big barn in the fields. We no longer had petrol to go to the fields in the car so I rode Gold. She was in the paddock and could be quite difficult to catch. I used a rope tied under my jacket round my waist. I talked to her as I offered a tit bit of food and got as far as patting her, then if I was quick I took the rope from my waist and put it round her neck and she knew she was caught. It didn't always work at first go, but it did in the end. At the field where the barn was she could be unsaddled and her bridle taken off while she grazed, tethered. I then milked goats and fed kids. In the winter there was not a lot of milk to be had so what was left after a few kids had been fed I carried back in a billy can while riding. I did this a number of times. One day on the way back something near the memorial made her shy and then bolt. We were quite near the drive gate. I had a job to hold her and the can of milk. 1 lost my stirrups and put my arms round her neck to help me to stay on still clinging on to the can of milk. I knew Francis sometimes played in the drive near the stables and I was terrified Gold would run into him or hurt him so I shouted as loudly as I could "I can't stop. I can't stop" over and over again, as we came down the drive at an al mighty speed. Gold stopped abruptly at the stable door and I was most thankful to find that Francis was not there and I still had the milk!

The wonderful sewage system that went down the paddock became blocked. There was a manhole in the middle of the yard outside the stables. Geoffrey produced some flexible bamboo rods and rather reluctantly put on boots and an oilskin to go out to see what he could do to unblock it. It had to be a day when it was pouring with rain. Being a glutton for punishment I dressed suitably and joined him. What he said about the incompetent idiot who put the wrong things in the toilet and expected them to disappear doesn't bear thinking about. He was livid, partly because he was almost sure he knew which guest was to blame and partly because he didn't quite see how he could deal with it without proof. Of course he hated such a distasteful task so I said "let me have a go" and once we had emptied the actual manhole with buckets, as there was room for only one at a time in the manhole. I was soon left to get on with pushing the bamboo rods into the pipe as I stood there in the manhole in my wellies! Eventually it was freed. The problem was solved by such a song and dance being made about it that everyone heard about it including the culprit. It didn't happen again!

Once it was wartime there was trouble with the electric supply. They had their own generator in what was called the battery house. An engine was run which charged the batteries and there was always a plentiful supply of electricity. I don't now remember the reason, but it may have been that new batteries were needed and could not be obtained, but whatever it was the electricity could only be used when the engine was running. This meant starting it up at dusk and turning it off late at night after which candles had to be used. Needless to say I learned how to start the engine, so that if Geoffrey was out, away or for some reason not able to do it I could and often did. There was a special way of doing it. First put the fuel in. then turn a disc. Fit the handle in and turn it as if cranking a car. If it fired, take the handle out and adjust the disc. If you were lucky it could then be left and it would run smoothly for hours. Geoffrey managed to sort out how many hours a certain amount of fuel would last which meant it would stop and he didn't have to go out to it to turn it off.

When it came to my birthday in February 1940, I was twenty-one. Wendy had previously had all kinds of fanciful ideas about a special party for me. Of course the fact that it was wartime put a damper on everything so there was no party. By then there were no guests left either. Just about that time the vicar's son was home on leave. The vicarage was only just up the road and he took to coming most evenings to see Wendy. She taught me how to play bridge and we played frequently into the early hours. There was not much else to do, everywhere was pitch dark and petrol became so scarce, we couldn't go anywhere as we sometimes had done before to pictures or sometimes to a dance at Askers Motel.

Animals had to be cared for but as far as possible during daylight hours. It was coming to the end of an era. Financially Wendy and Geoffrey could not keep going without guests. So many things had happened during the three years that I was there that many are forgotten. So many people came and went, both guests and staff. Some I can't put names to but I do remember.

A family by the name of Carter had been friends of Wendy and Geoffrey when they lived in Surrey. They came a number of times. They had a wonderful Rolls Royce which came into or left the drive almost without a sound, the engine was so quiet. Their daughter Helen who was about thirty years of age had been engaged for eleven years to what someone labelled 'that inadequate young man'. It was probably Zoe when she couldn't think of his name. Forever after he was known by all of us, by that title. My brother Peter met Helen when he visited and the family were staying there. He and Helen were married sometime after a courtship that was mainly carried on by correspondence. Peter was away at sea for two years. On his return he went straight from his ship to their wedding in the church. They had not seen each other during all that time. Helen was about seven years older than Peter. The marriage lasted only a few years, without offspring as Helen didn't want any children and Peter was keen to have sons to carry on the family name. I have no idea what happened to the 'inadequate young man'.

With just the family and about six others left, it was decided to sell up and move. The Bank of England had evacuated to a big park at Hurstbourne Priors near Whitchurch, not far from Andover. As Geoffrey had been made redundant from the bank some years before, he soon found he could get a job in the bank again.

About fifteen miles away the other side of Andover, Wendy found a large thatched cottage in the middle of the forest between

Ludgershall and Upper Chute. It had been a hunting box, for use when a hunt was taking place. It had three bedrooms and two bathrooms. Downstairs there were two rooms and a kitchen and a toilet. Out at the back there was a large enclosed yard with outhouses and a huge barn. Most furniture from Monkton Wyld was sold with a lot of other things that would not be needed such as linen and blankets. Somehow I acquired a bath mat which I still have. It is still good for many years and has been in regular use over the years.

The horses stayed up in the fields at first. For some unknown reason Sandy and I took Kitty and the trap and a lot of goats and their kids to the other side of Lyme Regis. We went down a ravine to where there was a very derelict old cottage with no windows or doors, in the middle of the wood where there had been a huge landslide many years before. We were not there very long but I can't remember how long. I know we cooked bacon and eggs while there. I also remember loosing some of the kids that were supposed to be following the goats and we had quite a job to find them. We both now think we must have been mad but as I have said Wendy could always get anyone to do anything she wanted when she wanted anything done and of course it was her idea. When she came to fetch Kitty and the goats, Sandy must have gone her own way. I went to the annexe for a while with my Father. While I was there I had a bicycle that had belonged to a twelve year old girl, who with her young brother had been guests at Monkton Wyld Court while their parents were abroad.

I used the bicycle to go up to the fields to see that the horses were all right or to go to get any shopping we needed. I found one day that the horses had got out and were along the main road that led down to Lyme Regis. Tim was always the leader of the horses and the only way to get him back was with a bucket of food. He would not be caught with a rope. I therefore got a bucket of food, which I let him have a taste from and then walked on. He followed and then I kept letting him have a taste. The other horses followed. There were five of them altogether, and eventually we got back into the fields. The next thing was to find the gap in the hedge or fence where they had got out and block it up. Finding the gap was difficult enough as there were quite a few fields all leading into each other and the horses had the run of all of them. Blocking off the gap was almost impossible as I had nothing with which to do it and no one to help. The local policeman came along. Someone had reported seeing the horses straying on the main road. I explained my predicament. saying I had got the horses back in but didn't know how I was going to block the gap when I found it. He not only helped me find the gap and helped me block it with branches but went round with me to make sure. there were no more!

While we were at the annexe my Father for the first time in my life shaved his beard off. I think he had always had a beard. He didn't stay without for long because he said he had a sore throat something he didn't normally have, so he grew it again. When we left the annexe my Father went at first to live with Furzey and his kind wife, which was in a cottage on the way to Axminster. I don't know how long he was there but I did hear later that because he spoke and of course understood German, he listened in to the radio and was often able to pick up German stations, but he would never have divulged anything he heard to anyone. Wendy had taken Biddy with her to Shaw Farm, which is what the cottage in the middle of the forest was called. She also had Robin who was another dog. He was a very young old English Sheep dog. Some years later I was able to have one of his puppies. I had it for nearly twelve years, but I had to give up my dog Toni. She didn't live very long. I had to have her put down. Once the horses had been fetched there was nothing for me to stay for. They went to Shaw Farm, there was plenty of grazing for them in front of the cottage.

CHAPTER X

THE STABLES

From the annexe I went to Shaw Farm but only on my way to a new job. I took the bicycle I had been using with me and was able to use it for some time before it was sent for. It was most useful. Geoffrey had found a job for me in the stables with the horses that belonged to the Bank of England. I didn't have to go for an interview. Geoffrey just told them about me and I accepted what he told me about the job. The stables were just down from the big house in the park, to one side of a large square yard. On the opposite side was the tack room where saddles and bridles were kept. In between on a third side of the square were workers cottages. Gardeners and groundsmen lived in them with their families. I was taken in at one of these cottages and given a room to sleep in. It was quite adequate, not that I was in it much. I had an alarm clock and had to be in the stables by half past six in the morning. There was just one little not very young man running the stables with about six or eight horses. I had coped with the horses that I knew at Monkton Wyld Court but this was a bit different. I had to learn to clear away the straw that had been the bedding for the night. Water and feed and groom the horses correctly ready for the first rides by seven o'clock. The riders were bank clerks and their families. With a war on and everything blacked out after dark there was little for them to do so the stables had been arranged specially for their benefit. This groom who was in charge had been a jockey or stable groom or both and he thought himself to be the 'cats whiskers'! He was very strict and wanted everything done to perfection. He did work hard himself and expected the same of me. Fortunately for me, something didn't suit and he was soon gone. In his place came two ladies. They had run their own stables but had to give up. The senior lady was aged about fifty. The other one nearer thirty. They were both spinsters and quite pleasant. They brought several horses with them so the three of us had twelve to manage. Two of the ponies were mostly out in the field and stayed out all night. The ladies certainly knew their job and both took out rides with experienced or complete beginners. I was permitted to have a ride when there was a free horse and a ride was going out, if I chose to. This didn't happen very often, much as I liked riding, as I was nearly always much too tired. There was a loft above the stables. Bales of hay and straw were delivered and put up into the loft. One of my jobs was to go up into the loft and throw down as many bales as were needed for the day. Grooming and mucking out, as we called it took a lot of time and effort. Every horse that had been out had to be groomed again before the next ride. One horse called Grey Lady always kicked when being groomed. There was one horse that was seventeen hands, a steeplechaser. He was a very comfortable ride but he bucked his rider off when he felt like it. He lived in a loose box. The others had their stalls. They were mostly ex polo ponies. There were two ponies suitable for children to ride, one was a cob a sturdy reliable animal, very good for children. They usually came on Saturday mornings or Sundays. I got to taking some of the children's rides by walking along side and leading the pony. A lot of time was spent cleaning the tack. Unless horses were going out again at once when they came in, saddles and bridles had to be taken off, carried across the yard to the tack room and hung up after the bit had been washed in a bucket of water. There were not so many rides during the day as in the early morning or during the evening while it was summer, or at the weekends. One polo pony became incurably lame. The vet came and said he should be put down. I won't give you more than one guess as to who held his halter while the vet performed his distasteful task. Not something I would like to do twice! The rides were round the park, so rarely on the road, except the road that ran from the gate to the house. Sometimes they were in the field that was within the park. This was where a few jumps were set up. I tried jumping a few times and found I could manage to jump across a stream. However when it came to jumping a fence, I was not so good. Once or twice I was all right, but after falling off I was not keen to try again. We had meal breaks at fairly regular times and two hours off during the day, but work went on into the evening until it was dark as after the last rides horses all had to be rubbed down, watered and fed and bedding put down for them for the night. My two hours off always flew. I was so tired that except for writing a letter or two and reading a bit there was no time for anything else. Meals were about half a mile across the park in a Lyons canteen specially built for the bank. It was self service and we were treated to whatever was on the menu, the same as the clerks and other members of staff. After the first rides we went for breakfast and could take one hour. It took nearly half that time to walk there and back. A few of the rides were taken by bank staff during their midday break, so we had to fit our hour for a midday meal as and when we could. There was also an evening meal. Again we went when we could. At four o'clock in the afternoon there was a cup of tea to be had in the kitchen of the big house. Part of the house had offices in it and those who were there came to the kitchen for a cup of tea and to save such a long walk for us, we did too. Most people worked in specially built huts in the park near enough for them to go to the canteen. They had huts to sleep in too. Some of the families had billets in nearby villages. Just occasionally I saw Geoffrey at teatime in the kitchen. He couldn't get home during the week but was home at weekends. I had two days off in the middle of the week on alternate weeks. The break was from noon to noon. I cycled the fifteen miles to Shaw Farm each time so I didn't see Geoffrey at any other time. When I arrived at Shaw Farm, Lesley who had been looking after the three children went to spend two nights with her friend Helen Harvey who was in her cottage in the New Forest. I took over looking after the children while Lesley was gone, as Wendy was working for the Forestry Commission as a foreman. She had at least one young man who was a conscientious objector and was working in the forest staying at Shaw Farm. Others came at times to visit. Michael was there on leave at one time when I was there. If there were not enough bedrooms, there were outhouses that could be slept in. Some of the outhouses had goats and kids in them. Buntub, who had come to Shaw Farm with Wendy and Geoffrey, saw to the goats. She took the whole herd for walks through the forest and they followed her quite happily feeding to a certain extent as they went along. There were quite a lot of kids too. I actually counted seventeen at one time.

When going to or from Shaw Farm I could go to shops in Andover, as I had to go through that way if I needed to. But I didn't often do that. Mother wanted to give me a late twenty-first birthday present which was something special that I wanted so I was to get it myself and she paid for it. I chose a travelling rug and some leather straps with a handle. I could then wrap all sorts of things in the rug, thread the straps through the handle and fasten them round the packed rag. It was most useful at times when travelling. In years to come, the moths had rather a lot of the rug but at least one of the straps and the handles are still in my possession. I bought them in Andover. There was no social life to be had during the six months I was at the stable. At that age it was something I felt I could do with. I enjoyed the horses but had very little to do with the riders so didn't get to know any of them. Sometimes we chatted to whoever happened to be at the table at meal times. With long tables and everyone sitting where they liked and people coming and going at no set time, one didn't very often come up against the same person more than very occasionally so there was no chance to get to know anyone. The park was vast and lovely, but I neither wanted to go for walks alone or needed to for exercise as I had more than enough doing the work in the stables and walking across for meals three times each day. Though at first I could use the bicycle. The highlight of my time at the stables was being able to go to Shaw Farm for my two days off. Latterly I had to use a bus to go to Andover and get another from Andover to go to Ludgershall and then had a long walk through the forest to get to Shaw Farm. Very trying but the only way it could be done. When I got there, there was Lesley to see briefly, unless she had left early and I would find Buntub holding the fort with the children. Wendy was there in the evening and invariably there was someone else. At least it broke the monotony of work and more work and I really did enjoy the children.

Plate Titles

Section Seven

53) 1933. Victor aged sixteen.

54) 1940. Edith and her brother Brian.

55) 1940. Victor in uniform.

56) 1941. Michael in flying uniform.

57) 1941. Victor's Aunt Amy with nephew Johnnie at Barnstaple.

58) 1941. Peter in uniform.

59) 1942. John, Amy, Johnnie, Victor and me at Barnstaple.

60) 1942. Johnnie.

61) 1942. Me with Sylvia, Grandpa and Mother in her garden.

62) 1942. Mum and Dad.

63) 1942. Me and Victor riding at Shaw Farm.

64) 1942. Lesley and the children at Shaw Farm.

65) Bantams and goats.

66) Me with some kid goats.

CHAPTER XI

I JOINED THE WRENS

People generally were by then saying that women were soon to be conscripted into the forces. The general consensus was that once they started to do that there would be no choice as to which of the services one would have to join. The last thing I wanted was to be recruited into the army and I can't say that the airforce appealed to me. So with brothers in the navy and fleet air arm respectively it had to be the wrens. This meant that I must volunteer in order to get my choice. I did this and was soon on my way for an interview and a medical. The medical board found it hard to believe that I had never had any after effects from the diphtheria that I had suffered from at the age of four. However, a complete examination told them I was as tough as they come. I put in for motor transport as I so much enjoyed driving and had missed not being able to while at the stable. My second choice was coding because I liked numbers and thought they would be involved. I was asked many things at the interview. One of them was, "Can you cook?" I said that I could. My attitude to cooking was that any fool could cook, after all the cooking I had done at the guest house by just picking it up from whatever Wendy had told me. I was of course accepted and in no time was sent for and joined up. I was greeted by the Wren Officer in charge when I arrived in Portsmouth with, "I understand you are going to cook for us." You could have knocked me over with a feather. It was the last thing I expected to have to do but I was just told there were no vacancies in either of my chosen categories and they were desperate for cooks and stewards, so anyone who could fill that role, had no choice. I was given uniform, at least some of it. White cotton blouse collars and a raincoat and a black tie. Also a hat. Not the type the sailors wore. It was one with a rim and a black ribbon round it which said 'H.M.S. Victory' in gold block letters. That was what all those at Portsmouth had to have. They had no navy blue suits in the stores, which consisted of skirt and double-breasted jacket. I had a navy blue skirt of my own which I wore for some weeks and as it was winter and I had no navy blue jacket or pullover, for a while I wore a pale blue polo necked jumper under my raincoat until I was given the correct suit. I had to wait months for my overcoat so had to wear the raincoat all the time whenever I went out. I was also issued with three blue and white striped overalls in which to work. I was accommodated in the wren's hostel in St. Michael's Road. It was only a short walk from the Portsmouth barracks where I worked. I have no idea how many wrens were there but most likely well over a hundred. Some worked regularly at the barracks. Others like me had just been recruited and were waiting to be drafted to a more permanent station. The hostel had been a children's home so there were dormitories. I was in one on the ground floor that had thirteen beds in it. None of the other occupants were officer's cooks at the barracks like I was so I didn't get to know them. One girl who came on the same day as I had a surname similar to mine. We were all called by our surnames at first. At times people mistook one of us for the other. She was in a completely different category and slept in a different dormitory so although I saw her a few times in the sitting room I didn't get to know her either. In any case I didn't take to her. I found her a bit insipid. The bathrooms were just along the corridor, very dim and not as clean as they might have been. If you went early to have a bath you might find some hot water if you were lucky. I had no need to go upstairs as there was a sitting room and a dinning room on the ground floor so I have no idea how many dormitories there were. I had to be on my way to get to the barracks and in the galley by seven in the morning. We had our breakfast a little later. We had all our meals at the barracks when we were on duty. They were good. Off duty meals were at the hostel. They were not very special but I didn't have many there and we told ourselves and each other that there was a war on and we had to be thankful for what we did have. At work there were shifts. A notice on the wall told you which shift you were on and in which department of the galley you would work. It also said when each shift was on leave. I was put on a shift that had the next weekend off. When I was told I was on leave for the weekend. I couldn't believe it. "But I've only just got here," I said. It seemed that didn't matter if that shift was off and you had been put on it, you were off. I was told to ask for a train pass when I said I didn't have any money to take me anywhere. It was possible to get some free and some at a reduced rate. So back I went to Shaw Farm from whence I had come, as I had been there for a few days after leaving the stables. I think I took a train to Andover and a bus to Ludgershall. After that I had to walk through the forest which was all right in daylight. I had off from Friday noon to Sunday evening. I then did a week's work where I had only done a few days before. If you worked the early shift, you were off at three in the afternoon unless you were due to go on leave, then you left at midday. If you were on late you came in at midday and stayed into the evening. Days alternated but you stayed with your shift. This also meant that you had a good mid-day meal in the barracks every working day. I was only there about six weeks, During that time I had at least two weekends off and a whole week for Christmas leave so I spent that at Shaw Farm too.

The other weekend off was spent at Petworth in Sussex. Dorothea was by that time in the Women's Land Army. She was working on a farm, mainly in charge of a dairy herd that had to be milked by hand. The farmer's wife was quite happy to have me for two nights and I enjoyed it. I offered to help Dorothea milk the cows as we both knew I had done it before. One cow kicked and knocked me flying. Dorothea said she was sorry she had forgotten to warn me that that one was always a kicker! On the way back I had a somewhat unusual experience. Petworth was not very far away and I caught a train that should have arrived in plenty of time for me to be back all right and not be late. I was the only wren in the carriage and there was no corridor. There were four sailors in the carriage all due back in their quarters in barracks in Portsmouth. As the evening went on the train kept stopping for quite a long time. Everything outside was pitch black. In the carriage there was only the smallest of dim lights. At first no one said anything. Then gradually, in turn, we said we were going to be late back but consoled ourselves with the fact that it was the fault of the train. The train seemed to go backwards and forwards at times and we dare not look out because of the light. Eventually we were stationary for so long and we could hear nothing, even any voices so one sailor dared to drop the window. "We are in a siding," he said. Each of us looked in turn. We could see no platform and there seemed to be no one about but the sky in the direction of Portsmouth was an orange glow. Obviously no one knew we were there, still on the train. From the carriage to the ground was a huge step. They jumped out and then helped me. We definitely were in a siding at Fratton. We had about a mile to walk. I was glad they knew the way, because I didn't. At least we didn't need any lights. The night before while we had been away Portsmouth had had its first air raid. Many incendiary bombs had been dropped and there were fires everywhere. We marvelled at it but all agreed we had not heard any news so knew nothing about it. They left me at the end of the road I had to go along to get to the hostel to continue on their way to their quarters. I hope they didn't get into trouble for being late. I didn't but I couldn't make it out when I found every light out and no one about. Finally, I was challenged with "Who goes there friend or foe?" I hastily gave my name and explained that I had just come off leave and about the train. Whoever it was didn't seem to believe me at first but she did not really have much choice and told me to go to my air raid shelter. I had never been shown any of them let alone been told which one I was supposed to go in. The wren Petty Officer or whoever she was said she thought there was room in one of the shelters and indicated where it was. As I went in a voice told me there was bench opposite the door. There was. It was a hard wooden bench against a stone wall and I doubt if it was more than fifteen inches wide. There was no mattress, or pillow and no blanket. But I slept on and off on it for the rest of the night. It was January 1941. I was frozen. In the morning, I ran as I usually did all the way to the barracks to find one man, a Petty Officer cook frying eggs out in the open on a brazier which is an iron basket that holds a burning fire like road men used to use in days gone by. Everything was a mess and there was no electricity, or gas or water in the taps, though there seemed to be plenty on the ground where hoses had been used to put fires out. Gradually things were cleared up and most things were back almost to normal. I had in my few weeks there spent a week helping to make and learning how to make soup and sauces under the tuition of a navy petty officer cook. After dinner there was little or nothing to do, except sometimes chop carrots up finely to put in the soup, but we couldn't go till our time was up. I enjoyed being on the vegetable shift as four or five of us stood around huge deep galvanised sinks peeling potatoes and chatting even singing sometimes. The men and the girls all worked together. Some of the men came in from the ships that had docked. They were there one day and gone the next but they were a jolly crowd. I felt really sorry to see them go sometimes because we knew they were going to sea and some would never come back. I had one week in the pastry galley. We made plenty of huge slabs of pastry and made it into pies of various sorts. There was one day when I caused the Chief Petty Officer to roar with laughter. He had called out for some large joints of meat to be moved from one place to another. He had not said exactly who was to do it so I just automatically joined in. He had intended the men to respond to his call, and couldn't believe his eyes when he say me carrying a huge side of meat. Throwing bales of hay and straw about and such like had given me muscles to cope with a lot of things. Because I had enjoyed the camaraderie when doing the vegetables, I asked if I could do them again. The Chief was a good sort and said I could but had another laugh at my expense because he said no one had ever made that request before!

Back at the hostel one day I was in the dormitory when the siren went off. We had been told to lie flat on the floor in case the blast from a bomb caught you. I dived under the nearest bed as I heard planes going over. After they had dropped their load, all was quiet so I came out, when a leading wren came along and nearly hit the roof because I was not in the shelter. I said I didn't know which one I should go in and added that I hadn't had time. The all clear went before I got to the shelter so I never did learn where it was. There were a number of them out at the back of the building all with numbers on.

There had been one night when I had been to have a bath. When I returned I noticed my bed was not as I had left it. I was always particular about making my bed. I had after all had enough practice. I guessed that I had an apple pie bed so before attempting to get in I retrieved my hairbrush and then remade my bed without saying a word. What a let down! Eventually they asked me how I knew. I more or less told them that I wasn't born yesterday and could easily see that my bed had not been the same as when I'd left it!

CHAPTER XII

"SO DEEP IS THE NIGHT"

Quite soon after the weekend of the air raids I was drafted to the Isle of Wight. I was told I was going to Yarmouth and someone asked me which Yarmouth when I mentioned it. I had never heard of Great Yarmouth before. At least four if not five of us boarded the ferry to cross the Solent. It was a sunny winter day and lovely to stand on deck getting to know we were all going to the same station and getting to know each other. One became our Wren Petty Officer Paddy Land. We went to the Pier Hotel in Yarmouth, which had been taken over by the navy. There were wrens already there. We had a wrens hostel just up the road from the hotel, where we slept and could spend our off duty time. Paddy had a room to herself. At first I was one of eight in a dormitory on the top floor. There were wrens of all categories in the same room. At first I worked mostly at the sink in the galley at the hotel with 'Cookie' who was a leading wren in charge and giving the orders. We both cooked for the officers. The number varied though there were a few permanent ones. There was a Captain, a Lieutenant Commander, and several Lieutenants, all older rather than young men. There was one Wren Officer. There was another cook who cooked for the wrens and all the men of other ranks. About a dozen wrens and a few more than a dozen men. The wrens were stewards, writers or telephonists. Two or three were leading wrens. The men were mostly marines.

There was a sergeant, a corporal and three or four with three service stripes on their sleeves. All older rather than young men. The other ratings were either marines or sailors. We had almost all the same ones there all the time I was there. One man was in charge of the catering for the men. He came into the galley daily with the food he wanted cooked and served for the men. Paddy did the catering for the officers and wrens and saw us regularly, particularly at meal times. The men came to collect their meals and always returned with a dinner on a plate to be kept hot for whoever was on watch. He had to come and get it when someone else had taken his place and he was free to do so. Watches were kept round the clock by the men who were signallers. They were either on the end of the pier where they had a hut, or they went on a yacht that put out to sea to meet ships coming up the Solent. Sometimes they had to go on the Pilot Cutter. The ship where there was a pilot officer who knew the waters and would board the leading ship of a convoy to steer it safely into port. Semaphore was used. Also an Aldis Lamp that sent out a very powerful light that was directed to exactly where a message had to be picked up in Morse code. There was a Chief Petty Officer who was in charge of the stores. He had been in the navy previously and returned for the duration of the war. Some of the sailors kept watch and one was a liberty boatman. He was often to be seen waiting on the quay with his boat at the ready for anyone who needed to be taken out to a ship, or brought in from one. We had leave for a weekend once each month. Although we were off from midday on Friday we were not due back until midday on Monday because we were on the island. We also had a whole week every three or four months. Our actual duty times were from seven in the morning to about one thirty. When we had finished we could go. Alternate days we were then off duty until seven the next morning. The other alternate days there was a two or three hour duty to do in the evening. This worked very well. Sometimes in the middle of preparing the midday meal we had to leave everything to go on the pier to take part in being drilled by the marine sergeant. At other times we had rifle practice, also under his instruction. There were targets at the back of the hotel in the garden and we lay down full length on the ground aiming at the targets with rifles to see if we could hit them. I don't remember getting a bullseye though I may have done, but I did hit the target. It was not the first time I had aimed a gun at a target! Another thing we had to do was to practise fire fighting. This was at the wren's hostel. I was told that as I was big and obviously strong I must take the nozzle of the hose because it was heavy and run with it as fast as I could as the hosepipe uncoiled behind me. It certainly was heavy and I was very glad I did not have to do it more than a couple of times.

I found that most of the wrens spent their evenings in the local pubs, usually with the lads. Not many were off duty during the afternoons. We could do as we liked in the hostel as we had a sitting room. I often sat there reading or letter writing. However to get some out of doors fun, I searched and soon found a riding stable and when I could afford it went for a ride. The riding master was also a farmer and had a job of some sort to do with the Ministry of Agriculture. He was responsible for seeing cattle that came off or went on the ferry. I had booked a ride one-day when he asked if I minded helping him to round up the cattle in the field, while on horseback as he had a herd that had to go down the road and on to the ferry. I was all for it. Both of us on horseback managed to get them all together and going in the right direction. He then left his horse and got into his car, going ahead of the herd. I took up the rear and all went well till we were about half way along the road and I had some trouble making them go on. He asked if I could drive so when I said that I could, he said. "You drive the car, I'll take the horse." The car was a small Singer. I hadn't driven one before but I managed as I only had to go in a low gear down to the ferry, when once he had sorted the cattle he took over the car again and I rode back to the stable.

Another thing I found to do was on a farm. I went to the door to ask if they had any part time work. I explained that I was a wren with time off alternate afternoons and that I was used to farm work. They asked what sort of work I wanted. I told them I didn't mind as I wanted to earn a few extra shillings so that I could ride more often. I was given the job of dock lifting. There was an enormous field with corn growing in it. I could go when I liked. I had to report when I arrived and when I left. I was given a sack with a rope tied at two corners that went over one shoulder while the sack dangled at the opposite side of me. I had a two-pronged fork and had to dig as deep down as I could to weed out every dock I could see. They have very long roots so I couldn't get the whole root out every time. I went across the field row by row and at the end of the row I tipped the contents of the sack into the hedge so it was never very heavy. I don't remember the rate of pay but for a time although I found it very tedious I decided it was worth it. Two hours at a time was plenty to cope with.

I went swimming in the sea sometimes. There was quite a nice sandbank to go on not very far away and some of the men and some of the wrens used it. One day I thought I would go swimming near the pier. There was no one else swimming there so I just went in and found I was being shouted at by someone on the pier. I could not make out why so I shouted back asking if it was out of bounds, so to speak. That wasn't the reason for the shouting at all. There was oil floating on the water and whoever it was, was trying to warn me. No wonder there was no one else there! I came out to find my upper arms, shoulders and part of my back were covered in oil. Even with some help, I had a terrible job to get rid of it. At least I was able to get rid of it from my costume, which was a maroon coloured, very good expensive Jaeger two piece. I was really rather proud of it. A Mother of children I had looked after at Monkton Wyld Court had passed it on to me after very little use. It was almost in front of being the height of fashion. No one wore two piece swimming costumes at that time.

Some time later on the captain at the station gave life saving lessons to wrens who wished to take part. We went out into the harbour in a small boat and swam from the boat while he sat in the boat. I did the course but towards the end when he was doing the tests for people to have a certificate the weather was bitterly cold and I had a shocking cold so I didn't go and never actually took the test.

There was one occasion when they were very short of kitchen or galley staff over the other side of the island at Seaview near Ryde. I was sent over for a couple of days to help out. I was thankful it was not for longer. Two things in particular stick in my mind about that trip. I was frying eggs and was ticked off by one of the other cooks for not scraping out the white of the raw egg into the frying pan with my little finger. She told me I was wasteful and more or less said. "Didn't I know there was a war on?" I was billeted in a very ordinary house and given a small room. It was comfortable enough but no one had warned me that there was what we called 'ack ack' guns on the hill behind the house. I could hear planes going over, once I was in bed and the guns being fired. I could also hear all the shrapnel falling into the sea. There was a lot of it and it made a lot of noise. I scarcely slept a wink because I wondered how long it would be before the shrapnel would fall on the roof of the house I was in, which was right opposite where the sea was. I didn't want to go down to ask people I didn't really know. I had no idea that they were used to it and it would never fall on the house. I dived under the bed clothes at the sound and kept coming up to listen and find out if anything else was going on. It hadn't occurred to the people of the house that I wouldn't know about the shrapnel. In the morning, I looked in the mirror feeling decidedly the worse for wear and found to my horror a couple of grey hairs that hadn't been there before. I thought that was a bit much at the age of twenty-two!

When I had been in Yarmouth for about three or four months. 'Cookie' was drafted to another station and I was made up to leading wren. I then had another wren to help me. She was a very young girl but a good worker. This meant that I no longer slept in the dormitory but shared a room with just one other leading wren who was a telephonist. Quite a few of them worked at a switchboard that was in the foyer of the hotel. They were connected to another small one on the end of the pier in the hut where the men worked. This also meant that I had a rise in pay from two shillings a day to three shillings a day. It was paid weekly. We had to line up for it and step forward when our names were called.

I put on a lot of weight because I had a habit of eating all the left overs that couldn't be used. However I decided that it was not a very good idea so I put myself on a diet of my own making. Black coffee and no pastry, other sweet things or potatoes. Nothing fried. Only meat, fish, fruit and veg. I soon took the weight off.

I thought I would like a commission. I fancied the idea of being a wren officer. Many people who put in for it were successful so why shouldn't I be? My brother Peter said he would put a word in for me, but he took so long that I changed my mind later and told him not to bother. Whenever I had leave I nearly always went to Shaw Farm as I was always welcome and enjoyed looking after the children to give Lesley a break and to help with the goats, or ride the horses. I rode Tim horse one day to do some hopping in Ludgershall. I was nearly swept off under the branches of trees in the woods. I did go to see Mother but London was not a safe place to be in. Mother was an air raid warden and once when I was there the siren went. She donned her tin hat and rushed off picking up a few bits she had put ready that she might need as she went, but the all clear went in no time and she was back as quickly as she had gone. She had by then moved to another flat, which was also in Winchmore Hill and was teaching in a local school. She was at that flat for many years.

Winifred was teaching in Woking where she lived with her son John who was four years old and Lewis who manned a barrage balloon somewhere, so may not have been at home all the time. My Father also went to live with Winifred in Woking.

Sylvia had done a midwifery course after her training and was at the North Middlesex Hospital where she saw and dealt with a lot of casualties in a very overcrowded ward, where there were beds all down the middle as patients came in after heavy air raids. She told of one time when she went to remove what she thought were hair pins or curlers from a patients head and found it was slivers of shrapnel embedded in the scalp. Sylvia had also been out on the district doing some midwifery work.

Dorothea was still in the Land Army in Petworth as far as I know until May 1943. She was engaged to Ray for a number of years but they were able to be married once Ray had been ordained so I think that must have been when she left. I am sure they were able to see each other from time to time up to then.

Peter was at sea so I didn't see him until after he was married which I think was early in 1942 and I think he then went to sea again but I am not sure. Michael was in Canada where he was training. He was in the Fleet Air Arm. so I didn't see much of him.

In June 1941 there was a big service dance held in Newport on the Isle of Wight. Almost everyone went. I was persuaded to because I was unattached and I was asked if I would take the raffle prizes round on a tray which I had fixed by a strap round my neck. This I agreed to do. While I was there I suddenly heard Victor who was on the stage singing, "So deep is the night," not a song I had heard before. I stood riveted to the spot with my eyes nearly popping out of my head. I couldn't believe that he could have such a wonderful tenor voice. I had of course seen him before when he had been into the galley to fetch his dinner after coming off watch, but not really spoken to him. In fact 'Cookie' had warned me off him, because she told me he had false teeth. That was a big laugh. He had all his own teeth and they were very good so I don't know where she got that idea from! All the sailors, marines and other men had to pass through our galley every time they wanted to go out or come back in so we saw them all passing through at times. I there and then decided that next time I saw Victor going through the galley I would speak to him. We had a few quite long conversations after I had told him how much I had enjoyed his singing. I was usually sitting at the table and he was standing at the door, so that he could be on his way if anyone came along as they were not supposed to dilly dally in, the galley. It was not long before we arranged to go for a walk. When I went off duty to change out of my uniform into my green corduroy trousers and hacking jacket which I wore whenever I could I said I'd meet him down a certain lane. I rushed off and knowing I was ahead of him, I climbed over a gate and hid in a field to watch him go by. When he came back I jumped out with a "Boo!" That was the start of many walks. We happened to have the same afternoons off so we soon extended them to picnics and going up on Tennyson's Down where his monument is and where I had been for a number of rides on the horses. Sometimes we went to the pictures afterwards in Freshwater. One of note was Noel Coward's Bitter Sweet. At other times we went on to a dance. I couldn't dance to save my life but it didn't take him long to teach me. He had been going out with one of the wrens who had been married but was widowed, she was I thought quite nice but often drank too much. She had just decided to finish with Victor so I came along just at the right time! At home Victor had had another girl friend but that relationship seemed to have petered out.

There were tennis hard courts in Yarmouth. The owners said any service personnel could use them. The wren who cooked for the marines liked to play and so did a few of the others. I found the hard courts much better to play on than grass that I had previously played on so I joined in but I found most of them played much better than I did, particularly Victor. Sometimes some of the army came to play too.

For the first two months or more after we had started to go for walks, my free time was not spent exclusively with Victor. We got on well and one of the main things that appealed to me was his sense of humour. Wendy once called it a sense of the ridiculous. Gradually I gave up things like dock lifting and riding in order to spend more time with him. I can remember our first kiss as if it were yesterday. Gentle, loving and sincere. His eyes rather than his voice said afterwards, "Did you mind?" Of course I didn't, I would soon have let him know if I had. At one time I found there were dances that he was not at, because he was on duty. There was an army camp quite near over the bridge. We were always challenged and had to show our passbook when we went there. At a dance there was one soldier who was very small and not so young who grabbed me for a tango. He wouldn't listen to my cries of "I can't tango". He was an excellent dancer and had me dancing a tango as I had never done before and have never done since, but I enjoyed it! Other men danced or tried to, with my two left feet. I got to know a few of them and became friendly with one. I thought I fancied him but once he got a bit close I soon found I didn't. Afterwards I realised I had felt sorry for him. He was a young man already a widower and had a sad tale to tell of a four-year-old daughter who had a cleft roof to her mouth. I spent rather a long time with him once when a lot of us were playing tennis. Victor was there. Someone else informed me that he didn't like it. My reply to them was that I was free and he didn't own me. It wasn't long before we were together again though, as soon as I realised my mistake.

There were plenty of dances to go to that were in the conservative club. There was also a snooker table there that Victor and other men could play on but I didn't. Some of the officers came to the dances and some of the local girls. One of them married a sailor and another a marine. Both couples settled to live in Yarmouth for the rest of their lives. I had had my hair cut fairly short as I thought it would be easier to deal with. Then I grew it again and learned how to put it in curlers. At the dances I often wore my square necked dress that I liked so much that Wendy had given to me. I also used powder and lipstick and wore clip-on pearl earrings. We arranged to meet at the dance, or rather inside the hall to save the embarrassment of who should pay. We always paid our own entrance, though Victor would get a drink for me. As a leading wren I probably had more pay than he did as a marine. There were times when there were concerts. Victor sang and sometimes acted a sketch. He also took over the drums sometimes to give the drummer a break. He had sung in many clubs in London before the war and played the drums. It was only at the local dances that we wore what we liked. At most dances we had to wear uniform. Sometimes we had a special coach to take us to a dance. One time we went to Brighstone to a camp in the south of the island. For some reason I was being given glass after glass of sherry. I had a feeling they were trying to make me drunk, after about half a bottle they found they weren't getting anywhere so gave up. At another dance, Victor had had more than was good for him so I took him to The Cabin to give him some strong black coffee before escorting him to the door of the hotel. The Cabin was a very small sitting room on the ground floor of the wren's hostel. It was intended for the use of P.O. Wrens and Leading wrens. It was rarely used except by me. We could have a friend in there so Victor often came in there. It had to be entered from the outside, as it had previously been a lock up shop. The rest of the ground floor where the hostel was didn't belong to the wrens. It was a chemist shop. In The Cabin there were a few chairs, a table and a four hundred-piece jigsaw. We spent a lot of time doing the jigsaw when it was too wet for comfort outside. On a few occasions Paddy our only P.O. used it and had a friend who was an older officer in there with her. We didn't encroach when they were there. We liked Paddy, I think everyone did.

There was a local district nurse who was also the midwife who invited service people to her home for tea sometimes. She often invited us once she had heard Victor sing as she could accompany him on the piano and enjoyed doing it. He couldn't read music but knew endless songs and could learn a new one very quickly. He always sang to me as we danced, as there was rarely a tune that he didn't know the words of. The men working on the pier had fishing lines out and caught many fish, which they had for their tea. They also set lobster pots and caught a number of lobsters. Victor was always very enthusiastic about the fish and the lobsters.

The men all had to do a lot of cleaning and washing and ironing of some of their clothes. Their boots had to shine till they could see their faces in them. Talk about 'spit and polish'. Victor was most particular about how well he was turned out to the last button that must be highly polished. He told me that, if he had known what hard work scrubbing was he would never have let his Mum do so much. He was never afraid of hard work. He saw me cutting up rhubarb in the galley one day. He walked over to me and said "Here let me do it for you, I'll show you how!" It was all done almost before you could say "knife"! I won't pretend that I hadn't been hoping for some years to find a husband. I wanted to get married and have a family. I had a few ideas about what qualities the man in my life should have. I don't now remember all of them but Victor seemed to live up to most of them. Honesty was the first on the list and a sense of humour was high on the list, and a special love of children. Being a hard worker was another. By about September I was as sure as I could be that Victor was right for me. Just one snag was whether he thought the same about me. We both went to Shaw Farm when we had some leave together. I don't think he ever got over having to sleep in an outhouse next to where seventeen kids were housed. Wendy thought he was a very genuine person. She also agreed with me that he had a lovely tenor voice but he needed some training. Some people thought that because we came from different backgrounds we would never stay together. Victor was a cockney, born and bred within the sound of Bow bells. Few people who met him knew unless they were told. I have always been pleased that he came from such a lovely family. I couldn't have had a nicer Mother in law.

By this time I had learned a lot about Victor's life before I had met him, in spite of the fact that he often said he couldn't remember much about his childhood. It seemed that when he was about six he had spent most of his time in hospital, which was not far from where he lived. He went in for one thing and then caught something else while he was there so had to stay in longer and then caught something else, so still couldn't go home. When he was at home there was so little room that they had to sleep three in a bed and had mostly coats rather than blankets to keep them warm. From all accounts Mum was extremely particular about everyone and everything being clean which I am sure was so. There was a loo out at the back of where he lived in a yard that had to be shared. They lived on the one ground floor. Others occupied upstairs. There was Mum, Dad and six children. The street was the playground, where they played football or cricket and used the wall at the end of the street for a goal or stumps. When he was quite small, Dad had him in the pub, where he put him on the counter to sing. He was in the church choir all his school days 'til at a late age his voice broke. Then he rested it for two years before going to clubs to sing with a band. His first school was next door so he needed no more than a minute to get there. By the time he was thirteen, he was at the top of the school but couldn't leave until he was fourteen so spent time filling inkpots or doing other odd jobs. He won a scholarship. But it couldn't be taken up because uniform and books that were needed would have to be paid for and there was nothing to spare for that. Dad worked for the gaslight and Coke Company. Victor won a place at the Technical College and had a grant for uniform for that. At sixteen and a half in the middle of doing a course in electrical engineering pupils were told there would be no jobs at the end of the course and if anyone could find a job of any sort they should take it and leave. Dad got him into his firm as an apprentice where he did a three-year course and qualified as a gas fitter with a City and guilds diploma. He went out on the district as a mate to a much older man for a few years and then soon after war broke out he was called up. He chose, and managed to get into the marines in 1940.

In November 1941 I went on weekend leave to Shaw Farm on my own. I had to go in wellington boots because by then the tracks through the forest were so deep with mud I couldn't walk through them in anything else. When I returned it was in the evening when the ferry docked and pitch dark. Victor was there on the quay as I came off to meet me. His first words to me were as he gave me a loving hug and a kiss. "Never again", never again what?" I asked. "I'm never going to let you out of my sight again." he said. Then I knew he thought the same as I did, and we didn't look back. We talked vaguely about being engaged but it wouldn't do to make it official, as it would be talked about. The authorities were inclined to draft one if they thought two people were getting together, so we made as sure as we could that no officers got to know.

Plate Titles

Section Eight

67) 1942. May 23rd, Victor and I as we came out of the church.

68) 1942. The Wedding Cake with the 'Bells' decoration.

69) 1942. Victor and me cutting the cake.

70) 1942. Bill, Dad, Mum, Victor, Me, Mother and Michael.

71) 1942. Everyone in Mother's garden after the Wedding.

72) 1942. John Budding and Peter Woollard playing, after the Wedding.

CHAPTER XIII

VISITING RELATIONS

Somehow by exchanging with someone we always had our leave at the same time from then on. I have a vague recollection of visiting Winifred and my Father but I don't remember exactly when. I know we visited Mother. Without her saying so in so many words I had the feeling that she didn't really approve. However she practised what she preached. 'If you can't say anything nice about someone don't say anything at all' is what she had always told us. Her first remark about Victor when he arrived but he had gone to wash his hands was, "Isn't he handsome?" "0h." I said, "I suppose he is, I had never thought of that". I certainly had never given it a thought but how right she was. Personality was much more important to me than looks and I had the added bonus of that lovely voice. When Victor took his jacket off to sit at table, he had braces showing. Mother didn't like to see braces showing at the table so asked him to put his jacket on again. He did as he was asked but I know he thought it quite odd. Apart from that there were no complaints.

Later we visited Victor's eldest sister Amy. She and her husband John with their small son Johnnie had been evacuated to a farm near Barnstable. I slept in the big bed with Amy in their bedroom cum living room. Victor had a bed in the landing and John slept downstairs somewhere while we were there, Johnnie of course was in with us in a cot. Everyone was most kind including the farmer and his wife. Amy managed to cook a good meal for us. Victor was her favourite brother. She had spent a lot of time looking after him when he was small. We visited Mum and Dad. They had also been evacuated from London where they had lived after being bombed out. They were in Glastonbury and Doris, Victor 's youngest sister lived with them. They had no room for me to sleep so hoped I wouldn't mind sharing a double bed with his other sister who was billeted in a house not far from them. Jenny was married to Frank but he was in the air force in the Middle East. Jenny had been evacuated and worked in Street at Clark's shoe factory. Dad worked for Clark's too. I was quite happy to share with Jenny. When Mum asked about my family. Victor told her I was born and brought up in a boy's boarding school. She then asked if my Father had been the caretaker. She couldn't believe her own ears when we said it was his school so he was the headmaster! We were by then very much in love and I think it must have shown. I was taken to friend's houses and others and introduced as "Our Vic's young lady". Jenny told me about Frank. Actually Victor did as well because they had been good friends, playing tennis and snooker and so on. I am not quite sure how it came about but I wrote to Frank. Jenny had said he was very pleased to have letters from home. He wrote back and we kept up a correspondence until his return. Both Mum and Dad were hard workers. No wonder Victor was too as were all the family.

We must have had quite a few weekends away together, with friends and relations. In the mean time we enjoyed a lot of time together. The men did twenty four hour watches of four hours on and four hours off. If they went on at eight o'clock in the morning, they worked for four hours on the end of the pier unless they were on a boat out in the Solent. The relief men went on at twelve noon after an early dinner and the two who came off came in to collect their dinners. If Victor went on early I caught a glimpse of him as he went out. When he came back he took his dinner and didn't have to go back until four in the afternoon. The second watch then came off duty until eight in the evening. If they were off then, I was often able to say, "Good night" before Victor went on for the night as he was due down on the pier by ten o'clock. Even during the night they only had to do a stand by duty while the other man kept watch. They could not take their clothes off but there was a bed in the hut to rest on. One night he could rest before midnight and between four and eight in the morning, and on another watch, from midnight to four in the morning. Coming off at eight in the morning meant having breakfast, doing chores and then being free after dinner until the next morning. If they wanted to sleep out they had to get a pass otherwise it was a case of being in by ten thirty unless they had a late pass, for example after a dance or some such. The bed in the hut on the pier was used by all the men in turn. It had blankets on it. I don't know if they were ever washed. I know one man and only one, known as 'Solid' because he was not as bright as he might be, was also not too clean. There was a time later on when Victor found he had scabies. He wasn't the only one and 'Solid' was blamed. With the right lotion from the chemist and caught in time it was soon cured. Victor didn't have it badly. He passed it on to me and I had a really bad dose of it twice. I think the blankets were fumigated and it was got rid of. With Victor's watches the way they were we spent every possible moment together and had brief moments in between. There were opportunities for some canoodling, last thing at night in the air raid shelter which was in the garden of the wrens hostel. It was never used as a shelter while I was there. We almost never heard the siren go. We didn't go into the shelter, as it was dark and damp and empty. But the entrance was out of the cold or wet.

We had evenings in the Wheatsheaf, or the club near the hotel for use of service people stationed at the hotel. One marine called 'Lofty', had what we all called a squeezebox. He often played it and sometimes Victor sang. I spent Christmas 1941 on duty but we were off in the evening. A lot of us went to the Wheatsheaf or the club. We had drinks and music and fun. There was a raffle. Ted, a sailor won three little Toby jugs. I had always had a shine for him, though nothing was ever said but I suspected he had a shine for me. He gave me those three Toby jugs because he said he didn't want them. I kept them for years but eventually let them go. However, Victor liked Ted and he married a local girl so we all kept in touch with each other over the years. In fact Ted's wife and I still do.

The sergeant of marines had a wife who was manageress of the corner grocery shop. He lived out with his wife. The Corporal of marines was an odd job man or may be I should say a "chippy" as he did maintenance work. He often came through the galley saying "What's for dinner today, kippers and custard?" He was another older man who had returned for the duration of the war. It was not unusual to see him when he had consumed more than his share of liquor. I don't know where he slept as he was very much on his own.

I was always on duty in the morning unless I was on leave. I don't remember ever going into the wrens mess room to have a meal. I had mine at the table in the galley just as 'Cookie' had done when she was there. With Paddy Land in charge we could get away with a lot. She was only a few years older than I and as long as there was a good meal cooked on time for her to serve to the officers she didn't mind much what we did. She ordered the food from the Chief Petty Officer who was storeman and she was not beyond getting a little extra for some of us to take on leave sometimes. There was no shortage of food in the navy stores. When we had some sour milk once I hung it up in the larder in a cloth to make it into a cheese just as I had done at Monkton Wyld Court. It turned out quite well. The larder was a couple of steps from the back door of the kitchen across a very small courtyard. We had no deep freezers or even a refrigerator to keep things cool. We had a marble slab to put things on to help to keep them cool. A muslin cloth with beads round it to put over a jug or bowl. The beads as weights, to keep dirt and flies out, and a metal mesh cupboard to put meat and fish in to make sure flies couldn't get at it.

There was one officer who had returned after leaving the navy some years before. He was not exactly popular and was considered by most to be uncouth or even uneducated. We could never fathom how he came to have the position he had, because he never sounded an 'h' when he spoke. One day he came into the galley after fishcakes made with tinned salmon had been served to the officers. "Who gave you the idea of 'eating salmon," he said to me. "Eating salmon," I replied, with tongue in cheek. "We always eat salmon." I said. "Making it 'ot in fish cakes," he went on. "0h, sir," I said. "You mean heating it, I expect it was Petty Officer Land, sir, she does the catering," I said. He obviously hadn't liked the fishcakes but we had no other complaints. We cooked by gas. There were three gas cookers in the galley so there was plenty of room for the cook who had to cook for the marines and wrens as well as what I had to do. We had no quarrels. I had used a gas stove when I was only twelve and living in the 'Little House' but most of the cooking I had done was on the two Aga cookers at Monkton Wyld Court. At least we had gas at Portsmouth Barracks where I had learned to make soup and sauces.

Through the cold winter I was thankful to have the warm navy uniform coat to wear over my uniform suit. I also had a beautiful white square silk scarf, given to me by my Father. It was permissible to wear a scarf under the coat and I found it helpful to keep the white collar clean as well as helping to keep the cold out. When I sent things to the laundry they were usually given an identifying laundry mark which consisted of a couple of letters stitched on in cotton. These could be taken off if required. One laundry I used took to using indelible ink, so I was very annoyed when I found my beautiful white scarf had unsightly black laundry marks on one corner. I had that scarf a long time, but like so many things it was eventually lost. Another means of keeping warm, or attempting to, was a hot water bottle. I had never used one but found that with a very cold bedroom at the hostel where there was never any heat and a bed that had the foot of it under the window, my feet were always cold in bed. We had a little kitchen at the hostel and I was able to buy a hot water bottle in the chemist shop below us. I could boil a kettle of water to fill it, wrap it in a woollen scarf and put it in the bottom of my bed to warm my feet.

I am sure there must have been a few of the wrens and the men that I can't recall, though I do remember most of them and their names. One girl married a Petty Officer who was an engineer from one of the boats. One night well after dark he got hold of a rowing boat and some of us had a ride in the harbour near the bridge. I told him I had rowed a boat years before so he let me have a go at taking the oars. It seemed much heavier and more difficult, and it was much bigger than the one we had had on our pond at home when I was only ten years old so I didn't do too well. Another of the men who lived out and mostly worked on the boats was a Chief Engineer. He was a little man and seemed quite old to us. However, I doubt if he was fifty. We didn't see much of him but he could give any one a good game of tennis.

Plate Titles

Section Nine

73) 1942. Victor and me on honeymoon at Shaw Farm.

74) 1942. Victor with Dad.

75) 1942. Amy, John and Johnnie.

76) 1942. Me sitting extreme left with the Wrens and Stokers I cooked for.

77) Victor in uniform, before we met, with all those he joined up with.

78) 1943. Geoffrey and Wendy.

CHAPTER XIV

THE WEDDING

Soon after Easter 1942 I received a draft to go to a wrens hostel in Southsea that was just about to open, to take charge of the galley. When I told Victor and before he had time to get over the horror of being separated, I said, "So we could get married, couldn't we?" and added, "We are both due for a week off at Whitsun." I don't think I gave him a chance to say more than, "Yes." He was as horrified as I was at the thought of being parted. We were as much in love as it is possible for any two people to be.

From then on it was action stations. He had no difficulty in getting permission as one had to, from his Commanding Officer, The Captain. When I approached our Wren Officer, which I had to do to get permission, she was sceptical. Did I know what I was doing, did I really know Victor, was I sure I hadn't fallen in love with the uniform and why the hurry? Were all questions she asked! I was able to answer all of them so she had no option, but I know she didn't believe all my replies. I knew exactly what I was doing. I had spent many hours with Victor on alternate days and seen him in between. We had been to visit his family and mine, and stayed with friends or relations on all our leave for some months and I had no illusions with regard to the uniform as he wore mufti as soon as we were away on leave. The hurry was simply that we did not like the idea of being parted and our next leave, which was due at Whitsun, would be an ideal time. She obviously thought there was an ulterior motive for the hurry, which at the time didn't cross my naive mind. She met me just over a year later and was surprised to see the baby had not yet arrived!

Victor wrote to Mum and Dad and of course his sister Amy, and his brother Bill to ask him to be best man. I phoned Mother who concealed her shock admirably and agreed to have the bands read at the local parish church St. Paul's at Winchmore Hill. Victor wanted a wedding in the Church of England . I said I didn't mind which church. It was not Mother's church but she went along with it and said she would arrange a small reception at her flat but there was only room for family. We arranged to have bands read in the church in Yarmouth and were able to go together to hear them being read, once. In the event, two who were not family, were invited. Sandy, who our family thought of as another sister, was invited and came. Edith my special friend was also invited. She asked if she could bring her Mother. I wrote explaining the invitation couldn't be extended. I have never heard another word from her since, though I tried to get in touch. Whether she took umbrage or whether she succumbed to one of Hitler's bombs, I will never know. I have often thought of her over the years and wondered, but I was never able to find out. We had twenty-five all told in the end. Victor's ex girl friend was at the church with her parents as he had let them know about the wedding. Mother approached them after the ceremony and invited them back to the flat. My Father and my Grandpa who was eighty eight, were not able to come, I still have Grandpa's letter apologising, saying he was not up to it. Grandpa had met Victor as he was at Mother's flat one time when we went there. Victor's Mum and Dad, two sisters, Aunts and Uncle and of course brother Bill were all there. I had three sisters and Aunties. Lewis had agreed to stand by to 'give me away' if Michael couldn't make it in time but he did. Peter was not able to get there or Victor's younger brother Bob.

I was soon on my way to Southsea on the 29th April, the day before Victor's birthday, to where it was all wrens, except a not so young stoker. I can't say I liked it. I shared a bedroom with another leading wren I don't remember who that was. I had the top bunk.

I had a wren assistant in the galley with me, she was all right as a worker, but for no particular reason not my sort of person. I did make friends with another leading wren who was married soon after we were to a soldier. We had a very bossy Wren Petty Officer who thought she knew everything! There were about twenty to cook for. Some of the girls were quite nice. Most of them worked at the barracks or elsewhere. I spent hours writing to Victor every day and he to me. The only way to see each other was for him to travel across the island to Ryde and for me to go across from Portsmouth to Ryde on the ferry when we had our half days off. We couldn't afford to do it every time. From earlier in the year Victor had transferred his special pay allocation that his Mother had been having to me. Men could allocate a certain amount of their pay to another person and then it was added to for the benefit of the recipient. Victor had been doing this for Mum. When he found that his brother Bob was doing the same and Mum was saving Bob's for him. Victor also found that she was not saving his for him, so he decided that if I had it I would put it away in my post office savings book. This I did on quite a regular basis and by about the end of the year nearly forty pounds was accumulated. I have my old post office book that tells me so!

On Friday the twenty second of May, Victor came across on the ferry and I met him at Portsmouth. We went on the train to London and found our way to Mother's flat. She had arranged for a friend of hers who lived quite near to have Victor for the night. First we needed to buy a wedding ring. Mother said if we couldn't get one anywhere I could borrow hers. We set off at about five o'clock to walk from Winchmore Hill to Palmer's Green looking for a jeweller's. By about half past five we found one that was shut. It had just what we wanted in the window and we could see a man was inside, so we made signs to him pointing to the ring and to my finger and to the two of us. He came and opened the door and after we had explained our predicament. He let us buy the ring. It cost Three pounds!

The next thing we had to do was visit the vicar. The Rev. Lancaster. I didn't want to include the word 'obey' in the service as I considered a marriage is a partnership, and Victor agreed with that.

However, when we told the vicar, he explained that in the context of the wedding ceremony the word obey meant to agree to have a husband's children. We then explained that we had already discussed that. Victor had said that I would be the one to have the children, I should decide when so I agreed to the word 'obey' being included. In any case we both hoped for a large family so we saw no difficulty.

I think young people today think that because there was no such thing as the pill in those days, that there were no methods of birth control. As it happens there were plenty and we were not without knowledge. In the event I wanted a June baby and that was what we were fortunate enough to have, but I found one couldn't always choose.

On our wedding morning, Sylvia kindly brought me a boiled egg but I had to tell her that I didn't ever eat a cooked breakfast. It was Sylvia who had scrounged some very necessary ingredients in order to make a cake, as so many things were rationed and some quite unobtainable. It was a very small cake scarcely larger than a breakfast cup and we decorated it with silver cardboard bells that Victor's brother Bob had sent. It was all he could send as he was serving in the R.A.F. abroad. The bells were bigger than the cake.

Michael arrived just in time to accompany me. He had travelled overnight from Scotland. We went in the taxi to the church after everyone else had left but found we were a little previous so had to go round the block before returning to the church. Victor was still being interviewed by the vicar in the vestry on his own. We were both in uniform so the dream of a lifetime went out of the window. There was no white dress and we had no bridesmaids. Bill, the best man was also in uniform as he was in the army. But I didn't mind in the least. Mother suggested the hymns and we went along with them. One was 'Love Divine all love excelling'. I don't remember what the other one was. Back in Mother's flat we had the reception. I think there was plenty to eat with cups of tea and orange juice, and we cut the cake. I was so ecstatic, I felt as if I was walking on air, and it was not due to any alcohol as Mother was completely teetotal. She would not have dreamed of having any alcohol in her flat, much to the disappointment of some of the guests. It was a fine day so we all congregated in the garden for a photographic session. Some photos had been taken as we came out of the church but film was very hard to come by. Victor's ex girl friend's father was a photographer. If it hadn't been for him we would have had very few photos indeed. He took quite a number for us which we thought was most kind.

We left in the late afternoon. We caught a train to go to Andover. Some guests came to see us off but the only one I remember was Bill. I was so happy I was almost in love with the whole world. I thought Bill was a lovely brother in law to have. I had not met him before. I gave him a really smashing kiss as I leaned out of the carriage window to say, "Goodbye". I can't think what he must have thought!

We had money from some people for a present as so many things were rationed but we did have quite a number of presents. A breadboard from my Auntie Elsie and Uncle Ronnie is still in daily use. We had a glass fruit bowl from Victor's sister Doris, a pink set of glass jug and six glasses from his sister Jenny. I still have three of the glasses. Victor's Aunt Amy gave us six small silver plated tea, or coffee spoons. I still have four of those but they are very worn. Bill and his wife Grace gave us knives. Victor's ex girl friend's family gave us a very nice green cotton table cloth which is still in very good condition in spite of having quite a lot of use and having a tin of blue paint spilled all over it once and then having to be soaked in parazone after. Mother gave me a very nice peach coloured silky nightdress. I only possessed pyjamas. I had never worn a nightdress in my life! We left most of the presents with Mother for the time being as we had no room to spare in our cases, we would have no use for then at first and no room to keep them. The marine's mess where Victor was gave us a wall barometer and the wrens at the Pier Hotel in Yarmouth gave us a carving knife and fork set.

When we arrived in Andover it was pouring with rain. We took a taxi to go to Shaw Farm. The taxi went via Upper Chute which was where the nearest road to Shaw Farm was. We went past a bungalow that Lady Rutherford lived in and a house that was occupied by Lady Eccles and her children. At their gateway the road ended and a grass track went up to the top of a hill and down the other side for about a quarter of a mile to Shaw Farm. Half way up the hill, the taxi got stuck, it was so muddy. Victor got out to try to help by pushing and was spattered with mud on his best uniform. In the end the driver gave up. We put our cases in the hedge. There was no one about or likely to be, as there were no houses near and the track only led to Shaw Farm. We then walked the rest of the way. I had a letter from Wendy who had said we could spend our honeymoon there. She apologised for having to be away as she and Geoffrey were to take their three children to see her Mother before rationed petrol for private cars ceased altogether. She said we could have her bed, make ourselves at home and Lesley and Percy would look after us. Percy worked in the forest. He was a good friend, only a few years older than Victor. As he was working during the day time he was only there in the evening during the week, but the first evening he went with Victor to help carry the cases we had left in the hedge once the rain had stopped. I stayed to chat to Lesley, no one else was there even Buntub was away. Victor and Percy were gone ages. They had gone on to the pub at Chute for a much wanted drink before picking up the cases to bring them back.

Lesley was as usual, marvellous. She produced lovely meals for us and did everything else including seeing to goats and horses two cows and their calves, chickens and ducks and any other animals that were there. We had a lovely week of mostly fine weather, and spent a lot of time walking in the forest. We rode horses and helped a bit with the goats and a few other things. Victor only had one week off but I had a second weeks leave because I had been married. We took a room in Yarmouth for the second week in a boarding house run by the local taxi man's wife. It was very comfortable and Victor was able to join me on the days he was off from after dinner to eight o'clock the next morning. Then I went to see him when he came ashore in between.

At the end of the week I had to return to the wrens hostel in Southsea. I didn't find that much fun and spent most of my time when off duty writing to Victor and was able to look forward to a letter from him each day.

Whenever we could we met in Ryde. There was not a lot to do in Ryde but we found fields up out of the town where we could picnic and of course canoodle! We always had to wear uniform, which just sometimes had an advantage. It was raining one day and we were at a loss to know where we could spend the three or four hours that we had. We asked at a boarding house if they could give us some tea. The lady took pity on us as we were in uniform and gave us a bedroom for the afternoon, which was not really what we had asked for. There was a table and chairs in the room and she served us with tea! We did have a few weekends when we had leave together, mostly spent at Shaw Farm. It was the best place to go as we were away from everywhere and could do as we liked. Wendy was there but working in the forest. Lesley looked after the children and did endless other things. The Eccles children sometimes came over to be with Wendy's children. When Michael was there he visited Lady Eccles more than once. She always made him welcome. Buntub was back to see to the goats. When we had our summer leave we went again to stay with Victor's sister Amy who had not been able to come to our wedding. This time she gave us her bed and slept on the landing herself but Johnnie still had to be in his cot in the room with us, not that we minded. There was a war on and we were poor. Beggars can't be choosers. We felt so lucky to be able to be together. It was haymaking time and the farmer was gathering in his hay. I had done plenty of haymaking when I was at Monkton Wyld Court and had enjoyed it. Victor was happy to try his hand at helping with the hay making, so we both offered to help. Victor was quite used to being in the country as he had been a scout and had been camping every year for some time, which he enjoyed. It was wonderful to get into a shirt and a pair of shorts again just as I had done before the war. We worked away with pitchforks putting the hay that had been placed in rows across the field, on to the cart that was drawn by the farmer's heavy carthorse. We were well rewarded with a good cold chicken dinner with new potatoes and vegetables brought out by the farmer's wife for us to eat sitting on logs by the side of the field. Amy joined us for the meal with Johnnie. He had been in the field with us earlier. It was a lovely day so I stripped his clothes off, as he looked too hot. When Amy came out she was horrified to see him without clothes, and put them back on. I couldn't make that out, all the three to five year olds I had looked after frequently went without clothes when it was hot. The farmer let Victor sit on his carthorse after it had had all the harness taken off. Another time we helped with the harvest too when it was sheaves of corn that were in stooks across the field that we had to pitch on to the cart. Of course when we were on leave, away from where we were stationed, we wore what we liked. I had most of my clothes from before the war. My green corduroy trousers and a hacking jacket were my favourites. Victor had nothing at all, as his clothes that he had possessed, and I had gathered that there had been many, were all in his parents home when it was bombed. It was in London and was caught in one of the first air raids on London in September 1940. The only thing he was able to rescue, was his guitar that was standing against the wall near the back door and wasn't touched. He was able at some point to get a pair of grey flannel trousers and a brown tweed jacket, so he nearly always wore them when not in uniform. The men were not allowed to change when at Yarmouth or anywhere they were stationed. The wrens were and I did often, unless there was a service dance to go to.

At Southea I sometimes went to where there were a few shops and was able to buy two pairs of double sheets at about a third of their correct price because they had come from premises that had been bombed. There was nothing wrong with them and they lasted for years. While in Southsea I met one of the wrens who had been the steward for the officers at Yarmouth. She was quite a nice girl who had been brought up in an orphanage. She asked me to go to the pictures with her. It was not a thing I would have thought of doing, though I had been with Victor, and certainly wouldn't have gone on my own. We went to see 'Blithe Spirit'. It was so weird I still remember people sitting round a table that moved when they put their hands on it! Where ever we went we always had to carry gasmasks with us. It was a bit of a bind, so to speak but we got used to it. The threat was always there, remote it's true but that was the rule. There were not many air raids while I was in Southsea but if there was one we all had to congregate in the inner hall which was very small on the lower ground floor of the building. It was near the kitchen or galley as we had to call it, and except to grab a gas mask and something to keep one warm, there were no special instructions. I was glad I only had to go there twice and only for a short time as the all clear soon sounded.

There was one occasion when a pie dish was burnt when something was cooked in it. Try as I might I could not get it clean so I left it to soak when the rest of the chores were finished to have another go at it in the evening. Our fat bossy Petty Officer wren tore me off a strip as if the world was coming to an end. I couldn't believe it. Talk about the crime of the century! Another time, I was late reporting back for duty after weekend leave. I had been over to the Isle of Wight. The ferry wouldn't run because the fog was too thick. I couldn't swim across so there was nothing I could do! Our 'dear' Petty Officer would loved to have made something of it but she couldn't, as it wasn't my fault. The company of wrens only, I didn't find very edifying. I would have preferred mixed company. I had been an officer's cook but for some reason I cooked for wrens only. As the winter weather came along, having to go on the ferry every time to be able to see Victor was a nuisance to say the least. I became broody! I no longer thought I would like to wait a year or two, as I had previously thought, to start a family. Other people had families and managed, in spite of the war so why shouldn't I!

By the end of October, I felt sick as soon as I was amongst the smells of cooking in the galley. I felt more sick in the evening than in the morning. I never was sick. My taste in foods changed quite a bit.

The stoker was off for a week or more and there was no one to carry buckets of coke to each floor for the boilers to be kept going. The building had been flats so each floor had a boiler that served the radiators and hot water tank on that floor. There were iron steps going up to the top on the outside of the building. They served as a fire escape, but were also used by the stoker to take the fuel up to each flat. Anything to get out of the galley and away from the smells. I volunteered to carry the buckets up each day and stoke the boilers. I had done it before and thought nothing of it. In the event it was not a good idea but I was not to know. Because of my condition I strained my back, which resulted in a permanent backache for about twelve years when I had some very helpful treatment. In the meantime I had a very acute attack of scabies. The medical officer was sent to visit me and he sent me to the Portsmouth sick bay for wrens where they gave me a special bath that involved being scrubbed all over with a special lotion and having it repeated a few days later. The medical officer also arranged a pregnancy test just to prove I wasn't having anyone on a piece of string, and of course it proved positive. My visits to see Victor were curtailed while I was in the sick bay. I was in there about a week and Victor was able to visit me once for a very short time, as he had to fit in with the ferry times.

Somehow I managed to get some white wool. All babies were dressed in white in those days. I started to knit a shawl and made vests and pram suits. This kept me quite busy in between my duties. I had been at Southsea seven months, seven months too long. It was very different from being at Yarmouth. I had been in the wrens for two years all but a week. I wouldn't have missed it for the world even if I did have to cook, apart from everything else, because I would otherwise never have found my beloved Victor. They didn't take long to send my discharge papers through. I was given my discharge on compassionate grounds. It was a new era, but I could never have imagined in my wildest dreams the joy I was to experience over the next fifty three years with my, beloved Victor. I couldn't have asked for more. I couldn't get out of the wrens quickly enough to go to be with him. God moves in a mysterious way.

We found rooms in which to live in Yarmouth. I was thankful to be a civilian again

THE END